Zebra Warriors

ORGANIZATIONS AT THE FOREFRONT OF CONSERVATION

Sanyub S.

Mohammed Altaf Hussain

Zebra Warriors

Contents

INDEX

Introduction

INTRODUCTION

In the tremendous embroidery of ecological stewardship, where the mind boggling strings of biodiversity, environment versatility, and feasible conjunction wind around together, certain associations arise as encouraging signs and change. Among these, the Zebra Heroes stand apart as an image of responsibility, solidarity, and activity in the domain of preservation. These associations, all in all known as Zebra Heroes, have excited endeavors overall to shield biological systems, safeguard jeopardized species, and address the dire difficulties presented by environmental change.

Beginnings of the Zebra Heroes:

The expression "Zebra Fighters" typifies a different exhibit of protection associations that have embraced a particular and joined approach towards resolving natural issues. The starting points of this aggregate personality can be followed to a common responsibility among these associations to break liberated from the ordinary standards of environmentalism - where a solitary spotlight on one part of preservation frequently ignores the interconnected idea of biological difficulties.

Similar as the famous highly contrasting stripes of a zebra, these associations intensely embrace the intricacy of ecological issues, perceiving that powerful protection requires an all encompassing and comprehensive methodology. The figurative high contrast stripes represent the double idea of their central goal: the earnestness of activity (dark) and the expectation for a feasible future (white). Together, these Zebra Heroes navigate assorted scenes, from tropical rainforests to bone-dry deserts, working energetically to make a permanent imprint on the material of worldwide preservation.

Shared Standards and Targets:

What joins the Zebra Fighters is a bunch of shared standards and targets that guide their undertakings. At the center of their main goal is a guarantee to biodiversity protection, perceiving that the trap of life is interconnected and that the deficiency of one animal varieties resounds across environments. These associations are driven by a dream of a reality where nature flourishes, where biological systems are tough, and where the sensitive harmony between human exercises and the climate is reestablished.

The Zebra Heroes grasp the basic job of networks in preservation endeavors. They champion local area based approaches that enable nearby inhabitants, perceiving that feasible arrangements should line up with the necessities and goals of the individuals who share their homes with untamed life. The consideration of native information and the cultivating of associations with nearby networks are basic to their methodology, recognizing the abundance of astuteness implanted in conventional practices.

Notwithstanding nearby commitment, the Zebra Fighters stress the significance of worldwide coordinated effort. They are very much in the know that ecological difficulties rise above boundaries, and aggregate activity is basic to resolve issues, for example, environmental change, living space misfortune, and unlawful untamed life exchange. These associations effectively partake in worldwide gatherings, team up with states, and manufacture organizations with other protection elements to enhance their effect on a worldwide scale.

Different Biological system Watchmen:

The Zebra Fighters are not bound to a particular geographic locale or kind of biological system. All things considered, they structure a different coalition of associations committed to the insurance of a wide exhibit of natural surroundings and the bunch species that call them home. From the rainforests of the Amazon, where the orchestra of biodiversity reverberations, to the polar domains where grand ice sheets cut through bone chilling waters, the Zebra Heroes are on the bleeding edges of preservation across biological systems.

In tropical scenes compromised by deforestation, these associations work enthusiastically to safeguard biodiversity areas of interest. They utilize creative methods, for example, camera traps, satellite observing, and local area based protection projects to defend the rich embroidered artwork of life tracked down in these districts. All the while, in parched and semi-bone-dry scenes, where the sensitive harmony among widely varied vegetation is tested by environmental change, the Zebra Champions carry out methodologies for economical water the executives, natural surroundings reclamation, and the assurance of cornerstone species.

Marine preservation is likewise a critical concentration for the Zebra Heroes. Seas, the backbone of our planet, face heap dangers, including overfishing, contamination, and environment prompted changes. Associations inside the Zebra Champions network endeavor to lay out marine safeguarded regions, battle unlawful fishing, and elevate reasonable fishing practices to guarantee the wellbeing and strength of sea environments.

Imaginative Protection Practices:

One of the signs of the Zebra Fighters is their obligation to advancement in protection rehearses. In a quickly impacting world, where new dangers arise and existing difficulties heighten, these associations are at the front of spearheading arrangements. They influence state of the art advances, embrace information driven approaches, and team up with researchers, scientists, and nearby networks to foster methodologies that are both successful and versatile.

Man-made consciousness, drones, and ecological DNA investigation are only a couple of instances of the innovative devices utilized by the Zebra Champions. These devices improve observing, empower more exact information assortment, and give bits of knowledge into the wellbeing of environments. The combination of customary natural information with present day advancements embodies their obligation to saddling the smartest possible scenario to support preservation.

A Promise to Preservation Schooling:

Past their activities on the ground, the Zebra Fighters perceive the crucial job of schooling in forming a practical future. They are focused on bringing issues to light, cultivating natural proficiency, and motivating the up and coming age of moderates. Training programs drove by these associations draw in schools, networks, and online stages to convey the significance of biodiversity, the interconnectedness of biological systems, and the job people can play in preservation.

Through narratives, instructive materials, and vivid encounters, the Zebra Champions mean to ignite a feeling of obligation and a profound association with nature. By imparting an adoration for the regular world, they imagine a future where people are latent spectators as well as dynamic members in the continuous story of preservation.

1. **Definition of Conservation**

   Preservation, with regards to the regular world, addresses a crucial ethos of dependable stewardship and practical concurrence. Established in the acknowledgment of the natural worth of biodiversity and the sensitive equilibrium of biological systems, preservation tries to safeguard, secure, and reasonably deal with the World's different living things and their territories. As a multi-layered idea, the meaning of preservation ranges biological, social, and moral aspects, mirroring a promise to guaranteeing the life span of our planet for present and people in the future.

   Natural Definition:

   At its center, the natural meaning of protection fixates on the defending of biodiversity and the conservation of biological systems. Biodiversity, the assortment of life on The planet, envelops hereditary variety inside species, the variety of species in environments, and the range of biological systems themselves. Protection endeavors to keep up with this perplexing snare of life by forestalling the eradication of species, safeguarding normal natural surroundings, and cultivating the flexibility of biological systems despite ecological difficulties.

   In pragmatic terms, natural preservation includes a scope of systems, from laying out safeguarded regions and untamed life stores to executing reasonable land and asset the executives rehearses.

   Preservation scientists assume a urgent part in grasping the elements of environments, observing species populaces, and recognizing mediations to relieve dangers, for example, living space misfortune, contamination, environmental change, and over-double-dealing of regular assets.

Social and Moral Aspects:

Preservation stretches out past natural contemplations to embrace social and moral aspects. Native societies, for instance, have long held a significant comprehension of their surroundings and the significance of living together as one with nature. The mix of customary environmental information into preservation rehearses recognizes the insight implanted in native societies, underlining the interconnectedness of human social orders and the normal world.

Moral contemplations inside preservation include perceiving the characteristic worth of every living being and recognizing the ethical obligation to safeguard biodiversity. This point of view difficulties anthropocentrism — the view that people are the focal point of moral thought — and stresses the inborn worth of non-human species. Protection morals advocate for a conscious and impartial relationship with nature, recognizing that all species, no matter what their utility to people, reserve a privilege to exist.

Authentic Advancement of Preservation:

The idea of preservation has developed over the long haul, molded by changing cultural qualities, logical progressions, and an extending comprehension of the interconnectedness of biological systems. By and large, preservation endeavors frequently centered around the safeguarding of alluring megafauna or the making of public parks to safeguard grand scenes. While these drives were vital stages in recognizing the benefit of protecting nature, contemporary preservation has extended its extension to address the more extensive biological and social components of ecological difficulties.

The rise of the ecological development during the twentieth century denoted a shift towards a more all encompassing way to deal with protection. The comprehension that natural issues are intricate and interconnected acquired conspicuousness, prompting the reception of supportable improvement standards. Preservation endeavors progressively coordinated social, financial, and ecological contemplations, perceiving that the prosperity of human networks is complicatedly connected to the strength of the environments they occupy.

Preservation as a Unique Cycle:

Preservation is certainly not a static idea yet a dynamic and versatile cycle that answers developing difficulties and open doors. As biological systems face extraordinary dangers from environmental change, living space debasement, and the deficiency of biodiversity, preservation methodologies should ceaselessly develop. Versatile administration, consolidating new logical information and imaginative advances, becomes fundamental in exploring the intricacies of the Anthropocene — the period set apart by huge human effect on the World's geography and biological systems.

The idea of dynamic protection additionally reaches out to the acknowledgment that human networks are basic parts of environments. Supportable turn of events and preservation are interlaced, requiring a harmony between addressing human requirements and protecting environmental respectability. Protection rehearses that connect with nearby networks as accomplices, regarding their insight and enabling them as stewards of their regular assets, represent the dynamic and comprehensive nature of contemporary preservation.

Protection in the 21st 100 years:

In the 21st hundred years, preservation faces uncommon difficulties and open doors. The direness of tending to environmental change, safeguarding basic living spaces, and saving biodiversity has prompted a change in perspective in preservation methodologies. Ideas, for example, rewilding, which looks to reestablish normal cycles and once again introduce key species to corrupted scenes, and biological system based transformation, which centers around upgrading the flexibility of environments to environmental change, feature the developing idea of preservation rehearses.

Moreover, protection in the advanced age use innovation and information driven ways to deal with screen biological systems, battle unlawful natural life exchange, and draw in worldwide networks in preservation endeavors. Resident science drives, where people add to information assortment and checking, represent the democratization of protection, stressing the job of aggregate activity in tending to natural difficulties.

2. **Importance of Conservation in the Modern World**

In the embroidery of the cutting edge world, protection arises as a basic string that winds around together environmental versatility, social legacy, and moral obligation. As our planet wrestles with phenomenal natural difficulties, the meaning of preservation has never been more articulated. From shielding biodiversity to moderating the effects of environmental change, and safeguarding social scenes, preservation assumes a crucial part in molding a feasible and agreeable future for humankind and the normal world.

Saving Biodiversity:

One of the essential goals of protection in the cutting edge world is the safeguarding of biodiversity. Biodiversity, the assortment of life on The planet, comprises the complicated snare of environments, species, and hereditary variety. Every part assumes a one of a kind part in keeping up with environmental equilibrium and strength. The deficiency of biodiversity, frequently advanced by human exercises like living space annihilation, contamination, and environmental change, has expansive results.

Preservation endeavors expect to forestall the annihilation of species and safeguard their environments. The unpredictable reliance of species inside biological systems features the significance of safeguarding biodiversity. A different cluster of plant and creature species adds to biological system solidness, versatility to natural changes, and the arrangement of fundamental environment administrations like fertilization, water decontamination, and environment guideline.

Relieving Environmental Change:

Protection is a vital device in relieving the effects of environmental change, a characterizing challenge of the cutting edge time. Environmental change, driven by human exercises, for example, consuming petroleum derivatives and deforestation, presents existential dangers to biological systems and networks around the world. Preservation methodologies, for example, reforestation, security of carbon-rich environments like mangroves, and maintainable land the board, add to carbon sequestration and flexibility against the antagonistic impacts of environmental change.

Protecting and reestablishing woodlands, specifically, fills in as a strong environment moderation system. Woodlands go about as carbon sinks, retaining and putting away immense measures of carbon dioxide. Deforestation discharges put away carbon into the environment as well as decreases the limit of biological systems to ingest future outflows. Preservation endeavors that focus on the security and rebuilding of backwoods assume a pivotal part in tending to the environment emergency.

Defending Biological system Administrations:

Biological systems give a horde of administrations fundamental for human prosperity, an idea frequently alluded to as environment administrations. These administrations incorporate the arrangement of clean water, guideline of air quality, fertilization of harvests, and the support of soil fruitfulness. Preservation guarantees the proceeded with usefulness of biological systems, consequently getting these fundamental administrations.

Wetlands, for instance, go about as regular water purifiers, sifting contaminations and directing water stream. Rationing wetland biological systems assists shield with watering quality and moderate the effects of floods and dry spells.

Likewise, coral reefs, frequently alluded to as the "rainforests of the ocean," give environment to marine life, shield shores from disintegration, and backing fisheries. Preservation endeavors pointed toward saving coral reefs add to the flexibility of beach front networks and the maintainability of marine environments.

Social Legacy and Biodiversity:

Protection isn't exclusively about safeguarding the indigenous habitat; it likewise includes the conservation of social legacy interweaved with biodiversity. Native people groups, whose societies are well established in their regular environmental factors, are many times the stewards of biodiversity-rich scenes. The deficiency of conventional information and practices represents a double danger: the vanishing of both social variety and the environments complicatedly oversaw by native networks.

Protection rehearses that regard and include native networks add to the conservation of social variety and biological uprightness. Perceiving the worth of customary natural information, which envelops feasible land the executives rehearses, restorative plant use, and versatile procedures to changing ecological circumstances, improves preservation endeavors. In doing as such, preservation turns into a scaffold between social legacy and biodiversity, cultivating a comprehensive and comprehensive way to deal with ecological stewardship.

Financial Advantages and Practical Turn of events:

Preservation is an interest in practical turn of events, offering a huge number of monetary advantages. Sound environments support horticulture, fisheries, and ranger service, giving vocations to a huge number of individuals. Reasonable land the executives rehearses, for example, agroforestry and natural cultivating, moderate biodiversity as well as add to strong and useful rural frameworks.

Eco-the travel industry, one more aspect of protection driven monetary exercises, profits by the charm of normal scenes and natural life. Safeguarded regions and biodiversity areas of interest become central focuses for reasonable the travel industry, creating income for neighborhood networks and supporting the upkeep of these imperative biological systems. Protection, hence, presents a financial worldview that blends human exercises with natural prosperity, encouraging a harmony among improvement and ecological conservation.

Tending to Worldwide Wellbeing Difficulties:

Preservation assumes an unforeseen yet vital part in tending to worldwide wellbeing challenges. The interconnectedness between human wellbeing and the strength of biological systems is exemplified by the rise of zoonotic infections, where microbes hop from creatures to people.

Natural surroundings obliteration, untamed life exchange, and different types of environment aggravation increment the gamble of such infection overflows.

Preservation endeavors that safeguard unblemished environments and address the drivers of zoonotic infections add to worldwide wellbeing security. Saving biodiversity and keeping up with the equilibrium of environments decrease the probability of sickness transmission from natural life to people. By perceiving the characteristic connection between the soundness of biological systems and human prosperity, preservation turns into a proactive procedure in forestalling and relieving worldwide wellbeing emergencies.

Instructive and Helpful Worth:

Preservation fills in as an impetus for ecological training and motivation. Drawing in networks, schools, and people in protection drives encourages a more profound comprehension of the normal world and the interconnectedness of every single living being. Preservation training ingrains a feeling of obligation, compassion, and natural morals, molding an age of ecologically cognizant residents.

Safeguarded regions, natural life asylums, and preservation projects become living study halls, offering open doors for experiential learning and environmental mindfulness. Preservation stories, whether about the fruitful recuperation of jeopardized species or the reclamation of debased biological systems, move people to become dynamic members in the aggregate work to safeguard the planet.

3. The Role of Organizations in Conservation Efforts

In the powerful scene of preservation, associations assume a critical part in organizing endeavors to safeguard biodiversity, save biological systems, and address ecological difficulties. Going from global NGOs to grassroots drives, these associations structure a different embroidery joined by a shared objective: the manageable stewardship of the planet. This exhaustive investigation digs into the multi-layered jobs these elements attempt, looking at their capabilities, challenges, and the effect they use in forming the direction of worldwide preservation endeavors.

1. **Preservation Associations: A Range of Jobs:**
   Preservation associations work across a range, incorporating a wide exhibit of jobs and works. At the global level, noticeable associations, for example, the World Untamed life Asset (WWF), Protection Global, and the Worldwide Association for Preservation of Nature (IUCN) take part in huge scope drives, impacting worldwide approaches, directing logical examination, and executing projects in different environments.

   Public and local associations frequently center around unambiguous difficulties inside their geographic degree. For example, the Public Audubon Society in the US accentuates bird preservation, while the African Natural life Establishment focuses on safeguarding Africa's special natural life and environments. These associations are instrumental in fitting protection systems to the particular necessities and settings of their districts.

   Grassroots associations, working at the local area level, are profoundly implanted in neighborhood settings. These substances, frequently started and drove by local area individuals, address preservation challenges with an accentuation on local area commitment, practical occupations, and the incorporation of conventional information. This confined methodology perceives the basic job of networks in preservation and tries to enable them as dynamic members in saving their regular legacy.

2. **Figuring out Protection Strategies and Promotion:**
   One of the essential jobs of protection associations is to figure out and advocate for strategies that advance natural maintainability. At the worldwide level, associations draw in with state run administrations, global bodies, and partners to shape strategies that address basic issues, for example, environmental change, living space security, and natural life preservation.

   Preservation Worldwide, for instance, teams up with state run administrations and policymakers to lay out safeguarded regions, execute maintainable asset the executives rehearses, and incorporate protection into public advancement plans. Additionally, the Rainforest Establishment attempts to safeguard the world's rainforests by supporting for arrangements that forestall deforestation, regard native land privileges, and advance economical land use.

Backing endeavors stretch out past strategy detailing to public mindfulness missions and local area assembly. Associations use different stages, including on-line entertainment, instructive projects, and public occasions, to bring issues to light about preservation issues, gather public help, and assemble networks for activity. These promotion endeavors act as an impetus for change, cultivating a feeling of natural obligation and motivating aggregate activity.

3. **Logical Exploration and Information Assortment:**
   Logical examination shapes the bedrock of compelling preservation endeavors, giving the information base important to grasp environments, recognize dangers, and devise proof based systems. Numerous protection associations effectively take part in logical examination, teaming up with researchers, scientists, and nearby networks to accumulate information on biodiversity, environment wellbeing, and the effects of human exercises.

   The Untamed life Preservation Society (WCS), for example, conducts broad field examination to screen untamed life populaces, concentrate on movement designs, and survey the soundness of environments. The information gathered by such associations contribute not exclusively to scholastic information yet additionally illuminate protection systems and dynamic cycles. This logical establishment is urgent for recognizing key biodiversity regions, grasping species conduct, and adjusting preservation mediations to the advancing difficulties looked by environments.

4. **Natural surroundings Insurance and Rebuilding:**
   Preservation associations are at the front of endeavors to secure and reestablish basic territories all over the planet. Whether it's laying out and overseeing safeguarded regions, pushing for feasible land use rehearses, or carrying out reforestation projects, these associations assume a significant part in saving the honesty of environments.

   The Nature Conservancy, a worldwide preservation association, has been instrumental in gaining and overseeing safeguarded regions, protecting different scenes from deforestation, territory discontinuity, and different dangers. Additionally, crafted by the Arbor Day Establishment centers around tree establishing drives to reestablish woods and upgrade biodiversity. Through these drives, associations add to the safeguarding of environments, the counteraction of species eradication, and the general wellbeing of biological systems.

5. **Fighting Unlawful Natural life Exchange:**
   Unlawful untamed life exchange represents an extreme danger to numerous species, pushing populaces to the edge of elimination and sabotaging preservation endeavors. Associations committed to battling this unlawful exchange utilize a diverse methodology, consolidating policing, commitment, and global coordinated effort.

   The Overall Asset for Nature (WWF) and the Worldwide Crook Police

Association (INTERPOL) team up to battle untamed life dealing internationally. They work with policing, customs specialists, and nearby networks to upset natural life dealing organizations, uphold against poaching measures, and bring issues to light about the outcomes of unlawful natural life exchange. By tending to the underlying drivers of natural life dealing and reinforcing lawful structures, these associations add to the assurance of imperiled species.

6. **Local area Commitment and Economical Vocations:**
   Preservation associations perceive that the prosperity of neighborhood networks is complicatedly connected to the progress of protection endeavors. Connecting with networks as dynamic members, as opposed to latent partners, is a major way to deal with accomplishing reasonable results.

   Associations frequently work inseparably with neighborhood networks to foster protection procedures that line up with their necessities and yearnings.

   The Rainforest Establishment, for instance, teams up with native networks to safeguard rainforests and maintain land freedoms. By engaging nearby networks as stewards of their regular assets, associations upgrade the viability of protection drives as well as add to the prosperity and financial supportability of these networks. Supportable job programs, including eco-accommodating farming and ecotourism, offer elective kinds of revenue that lighten tension on environments.

7. **Training and Limit Building:**
   Protection associations perceive the significance of schooling and limit working in encouraging a culture of ecological stewardship. Instructive projects, focused on at schools, networks, and chiefs, intend to bring issues to light about preservation issues, construct biological education, and rouse a feeling of obligation towards the climate.

   The Jane Goodall Foundation, through its Foundations and Shoots program, draws in youngsters in natural preservation, empowering them to become advocates for positive change. By putting resources into schooling, associations lay the preparation for people in the future to take part in protection endeavors and become educated advocates for ecological supportability effectively.

8. **Cooperation and Associations:**

The intricacy of protection challenges requires coordinated effort and associations among associations, legislatures, organizations, and neighborhood networks. Protection elements frequently structure partnerships to pool assets, share skill, and enhance the effect of their intercessions.

The Preservation Stewards Program, a coordinated effort between Protection Global and Starbucks, outlines the force of organizations. This program centers around advancing economical espresso creation, accordingly defending biodiversity and supporting the jobs of espresso ranchers. Joint efforts between protection associations and confidential area elements empower the coordination of preservation standards into strategic approaches, adding to feasible inventory chains.

Difficulties and Future Standpoint:

While protection associations assume an essential part in tending to ecological difficulties, they likewise face a horde of difficulties. Deficient financing, political obstruction, and the unavoidable effects of environmental change present considerable impediments. Additionally, guaranteeing the drawn out manageability of preservation drives requires exploring complex social, financial, and political scenes.

The future standpoint for preservation associations depends on their capacity to adjust to advancing difficulties, cultivate inclusivity, and influence inventive methodologies. Tackling innovation, embracing local area driven arrangements, and upholding for strategy changes are fundamental parts of a versatile preservation methodology. Furthermore, associations should constantly take a stab at expanded variety and inclusivity, perceiving the significance of consolidating different viewpoints and voices in protection dynamic cycles.

D. Overview of Zebra Warriors and their Significance

In the domain of protection, a particular power has arisen, joining different associations under a typical pennant — the Zebra Champions. Representing strength, solidarity, and a pledge to comprehensive ecological stewardship, the Zebra Champions have risen above traditional protection standards. This outline dives into the starting points, standards, and meaning of the Zebra Champions, revealing insight into their special methodology and the effect they use in the worldwide battle for ecological maintainability.

Beginnings of Zebra Fighters:

The beginning of the expression "Zebra Heroes" lies in an aggregate craving among different preservation associations to break liberated from the impediments of conventional methodologies. The similarity draws from the famous high contrast stripes of zebras, mirroring the double idea of their main goal — evil act (dark) and expectation for a supportable future (white). The Zebra Heroes epitomize a takeoff from single-center protection to a more comprehensive and interconnected approach that recognizes the intricacy of ecological difficulties.

The term mirrors a guarantee to embracing the many-sided trap of biodiversity, perceiving that the endurance of one animal categories is interwoven with the prosperity of biological systems and, subsequently, the whole planet. The Zebra Heroes stand joined in their assurance to explore the mind boggling territory of natural issues with a striking, creative, and cooperative soul.

Shared Standards and Targets:

At the core of the Zebra Fighters' main goal are shared standards and targets that guide their undertakings. The focal precept is a promise to biodiversity protection, understanding that the soundness of biological systems depends on the variety of species, living spaces, and environments. This all encompassing point of view perceives that tending to natural difficulties requires an incorporated and cooperative methodology, rising above geological and disciplinary limits.

Zebra Champions stress the significance of local area commitment, recognizing that nearby networks are basic to preservation endeavors as well as have important information and bits of knowledge.

The standards likewise incorporate a pledge to worldwide coordinated effort, perceiving that ecological difficulties are innately interconnected and request aggregate activity on a global scale.

Different Environment Gatekeepers:

Dissimilar to preservation drives with a thin concentration, the Zebra Heroes structure a different union of associations committed to the insurance of different environments and their particular occupants. From tropical rainforests to bone-dry deserts, from marine conditions to polar scenes, the Zebra Fighters cross the globe, tending to protection challenges in assorted natural surroundings.

This variety mirrors a nuanced comprehension of the interconnectedness of biological systems and the requirement for versatile techniques customized to various conditions. The Zebra Fighters perceive that successful protection requires setting explicit methodologies that think about the interesting qualities and difficulties of every biological system.

Imaginative Protection Practices:

A distinctive component of the Zebra Fighters is their obligation to creative protection rehearses. In a quickly impacting world, where new dangers arise and existing difficulties strengthen, these associations influence state of the art advances, information driven approaches, and cooperative exploration to foster powerful and versatile methodologies.

Man-made consciousness, satellite observing, and ecological DNA examination are only a couple of instances of the innovative instruments utilized by the Zebra Heroes. These instruments upgrade observing, empower more exact information assortment, and give experiences into the soundness of environments. The incorporation of innovation with customary natural information represents the Zebra Heroes' ground breaking approach, utilizing the smartest scenario imaginable to assist preservation.

Local area Based Protection and Strengthening:

Local area based protection is a foundation of the Zebra Champions' procedure. Perceiving the fundamental job that nearby networks play in the progress of preservation drives, these associations effectively draw in with and enable networks. By including nearby occupants in dynamic cycles, executing reasonable work programs, and regarding native information, the Zebra Champions cultivate a feeling of pride and obligation among networks.

This people group driven approach improves the adequacy of preservation endeavors as well as adds to the prosperity and flexibility of nearby populaces. It lines up with the comprehension that reasonable preservation rehearses should consider the financial setting and goals of individuals who share their environments with untamed life.

Worldwide Joint efforts and Associations:

The Zebra Heroes expand their effect past individual drives through worldwide coordinated efforts and organizations. Perceiving that natural difficulties rise above borders, these associations effectively draw in with states, global bodies, and other protection elements to enhance their impact.

Joint efforts with nearby and global elements work with the trading of information, assets, and best practices. The Zebra Fighters influence these organizations to resolve worldwide issues, for example, environmental change, natural surroundings misfortune, and unlawful untamed life exchange. By working cooperatively, they amplify their effect and add to a more planned and successful worldwide protection exertion.

The Utilization of Innovation in Protection Endeavors:

Innovation assumes an essential part in the Zebra Champions' preservation tries. From cutting edge checking frameworks to information investigation instruments, these associations outfit innovation to accumulate exact data about biological systems, track untamed life developments, and survey the effect of human exercises on the climate.

The utilization of robots, for instance, empowers the Zebra Champions to direct aeronautical studies, screen distant regions, and assemble information on environment wellbeing. Geographic Data Framework (GIS) innovation helps with spatial examination, considering informed navigation in regards to land use and protection needs. The Zebra Fighters embrace innovation as a competitive edge, improving their ability to address natural difficulties with proficiency and precision.

The Appearances Behind Zebra Champions:

Past hierarchical designs, the Zebra Fighters are contained people — researchers, activists, moderates, and local area pioneers — who devote their lives to the reason. These people encapsulate the soul of the Zebra Heroes, showing strength, energy, and a profound obligation to ecological preservation.

Researchers inside the Zebra Fighters contribute important mastery, leading exploration, and creating inventive arrangements. Activists champion the reason, bringing issues to light, preparing networks, and supporting for strategy changes. Progressives work on the ground, carrying out projects, and teaming up with neighborhood networks. The aggregate endeavors of these people structure the foundation of the Zebra Fighters, driving change at both nearby and worldwide levels.

Difficulties and Wins:

Notwithstanding their honorable mission, the Zebra Champions face imposing difficulties. Deficient financing, political obstruction, and the unavoidable effects of environmental change present impediments to their undertakings. Also, the intricacy of preservation issues requests persistent variation and imaginative arrangements.

In any case, the Zebra Champions have likewise accomplished huge victories. Examples of overcoming adversity incorporate the recuperation of imperiled species, the foundation of safeguarded regions, and the reclamation of corrupted environments.

These triumphs act as encouraging signs, showing the way that aggregate activity and creative methodologies can have an unmistakable effect even with natural difficulties.

Chapter 1

The Genesis of Zebra Warriors

In the core of the African savannah, where the sun sets in a blast of orange and the breeze murmurs through the tall grass, a special and captivating local area known as the Zebra Champions arose. The beginning of the Zebra Champions is a story woven with strings of social lavishness, strength, and a profound association with the land they call home.

The Place that is known for Stripes

The Zebra Champions track down their underlying foundations in the immense scenes of eastern Africa, where the notorious acacia trees stand tall against the background of vast fields. It is in this land, where the skyline appears to extend on everlastingly, that the zebras wander openly. These magnificent animals, with their unmistakable highly contrasting stripes, turned out to be something other than occupants of the savannah for individuals who coincided with them. They became images of solidarity, solidarity, and an amicable relationship with nature.

Social Embroidered artwork

The beginning of the Zebra Heroes is profoundly interlaced with the rich embroidery of African societies that have prospered for a really long time. The people group that led to these fighters have consistently held a significant love for nature and its cycles. The zebras, with their interesting markings, turned into a wellspring of motivation for individuals, mirroring the possibility that variety isn't just regular however fundamental for the endurance of a local area.

Customs and functions were created to respect the zebras and look for their direction. Individuals trusted that by copying the soul of these eminent animals, they could take advantage of a wellspring of versatility and fortitude. This established the groundwork for what might later turn into the Zebra Fighters, a local area that embraced the upsides of variety, versatility, and aggregate strength.

The Ascent of the Zebra Heroes

As the networks developed, so did the job of the Zebra Fighters. The beginning of this novel gathering can be followed to a progression of difficulties and misfortunes looked by individuals of the savannah. Brutal environments, regional questions, and the consistently present danger of hunters requested a reaction that went past individual capacities. It was during these seasons of difficulty that the Zebra Champions arose as a bringing together power.

The older folks of the networks, drawing motivation from the zebras, imagined a gathering of people who could stand together notwithstanding difficulty. They perceived that strength lies in individual ability as well as in the capacity to move as one, similar as a crowd of zebras exploring the open fields. Subsequently, the Zebra Heroes were conceived, turning into the gatekeepers of their kin and the encapsulation of solidarity in variety.

The Code of the Stripes

Fundamental to the character of the Zebra Fighters is the Code of the Stripes, a bunch of rules that guide their lifestyle. This code underlines the significance of variety, participation, and flexibility, repeating the examples tracked down in the stripes of the zebras. Every individual from the local area is supposed to exemplify these standards, cultivating a feeling of having a place and common perspective.

The main stripe of the code addresses solidarity. The Zebra Fighters comprehend that their solidarity lies in their capacity to meet up, rising above individual contrasts for everyone's benefit. Similar as the zebras that structure defensive circles around their young, the fighters make a safeguard of fortitude that protects their local area.

The subsequent stripe connotes versatility. Life on the savannah is capricious, and the Zebra Fighters have figured out how to explore its difficulties with adaptability and flexibility. They embrace change as a characteristic piece of their reality, understanding that unbending nature can prompt stagnation. By adjusting to the always moving scenes, the fighters guarantee the endurance and thriving of their kin.

The third stripe represents variety. The zebras' high contrast stripes are a demonstration of the excellence of contrasts meeting up together as one. The Zebra Heroes celebrate variety inside their local area, perceiving that every individual brings a novel arrangement of abilities and viewpoints. By esteeming and regarding these distinctions, the heroes make a mosaic of qualities that invigorates their aggregate soul.

The Ceremonies of the Zebras

To support their association with the zebras and the standards of the Code of the Stripes, the Zebra Fighters take part in intricate customs that give recognition to their creature partners. One such custom is the Dance of the Stripes, a stylized exhibition that imitates the smooth developments of zebras on the savannah. Through many-sided movement, the heroes represent the solidarity, versatility, and variety that characterize their reality.

Another significant custom is the Social affair of the Group, where the whole local area meets up to share stories, intelligence, and encounters. This ceremonial fills in as an update that, similar to a group of zebras, the strength of the local area lies in the bonds manufactured through shared history and common comprehension.

Difficulties and Wins

The excursion of the Zebra Heroes has not been without its difficulties. The cruel real factors of the African savannah, combined with outer tensions, have tried the flexibility of this extraordinary local area. However, it is definitively during these difficult times that the genuine soul of the Zebra Fighters radiates through.

Quite possibly of the main test looked by the Zebra Fighters was the infringement of outside impacts undermining their customary lifestyle. The champions, nonetheless, drew motivation from the zebras, who have adjusted to changing conditions for centuries. Embracing the standards of flexibility, the Zebra Heroes tracked down creative ways of saving their social legacy while exploring the intricacies of the cutting edge world.

Wins for the Zebra Champions frequently come as collective accomplishments. From effectively battling off outside dangers to making supportable practices that blend with the climate, the champions keep on demonstrating that the Code of the Stripes isn't simply a bunch of goals however a no nonsense way of thinking that directs their activities.

Inheritance and Future

As the Zebra Champions keep on flourishing in the core of the African savannah, their heritage turns into a motivation for a long time into the future. The beginning of this uncommon local area, established in a profound association with nature and a guarantee to shared values, fills in as an encouraging sign in a world frequently set apart by division.

The eventual fate of the Zebra Heroes lies in their capacity to adjust while remaining consistent with their social roots. As their general surroundings develops, the heroes stay relentless in their obligation to the Code of the Stripes, guaranteeing that the standards of solidarity, flexibility, and variety are passed down starting with one age then onto the next.

In our current reality where the significance of congruity and equilibrium is progressively perceived, the Zebra Fighters stand as residing epitomes of these standards. Through their extraordinary beginning, social practices, and steadfast soul, the Zebra Heroes keep on making a permanent imprint on the embroidery of mankind's set of experiences — a demonstration of the persevering through force of solidarity in variety.

1.1 Historical Background of Conservation Movements

The foundations of present day preservation developments stretch profound into the chronicles of history, molded by a mind boggling interaction of social, monetary, and natural variables. These developments have developed over hundreds of years, driven by a developing familiarity with humankind's effect on the regular world and an acknowledgment of the need to save and safeguard the World's different environments. Inspecting the authentic foundation of preservation developments gives knowledge into the inspirations, key figures, and critical occasions that have formed the manner in which social orders see and connect with their current circumstance.

Old Protection Morals:

While the expression "protection" might be a somewhat late expansion to our jargon, old civilizations held their own renditions of preservation morals. In numerous native societies, a profound association with the land and a significant regard for nature were major parts of their conviction frameworks. Practices like reasonable hunting, occasional asset the executives, and profound ceremonies pointed toward keeping an agreeable relationship with the climate show early endeavors at preservation.

In antiquated China, for instance, the idea of "feng shui" stressed the significance of natural equilibrium for the prosperity of the two people and networks. Additionally, Local American clans rehearsed maintainable horticulture and hunting, figuring out the interconnectedness of every living thing. These early protection standards were established in the comprehension that human endurance was unpredictably connected to the strength of the regular world.

The Introduction of Preservation as an Idea:

The formalization of preservation as an idea picked up speed during the European Illumination in the eighteenth hundred years. Scholars like Jean-Jacques Rousseau and George Perkins Swamp started to verbalize the possibility that human exercises could significantly affect the climate, and that dependable stewardship was fundamental for people in the future.

George Perkins Bog, an American negotiator and researcher, distributed "Man and Nature" in 1864, a notable work that featured the connection between human exercises and ecological debasement. Bog's thoughts established the groundwork for present day environmentalism and preservation morals, stressing the significance of practical asset use and natural equilibrium.

Early Protection Endeavors:

In the nineteenth hundred years, as industrialization moved throughout Europe and North America, the effect of human exercises on the climate turned out to be progressively evident.

Fast deforestation, contamination of streams, and the elimination of specific species incited worries about the drawn out results of unrestrained turn of events.

One of the earliest and most compelling protection figures of this time was John Muir, a Scottish-American naturalist. Muir's endeavors were instrumental in the foundation of Yosemite Public Park in 1890, denoting a critical stage in the acknowledgment of the need to secure and safeguard regular scenes. Muir's works and support laid the basis for the protection development in the US.

Theodore Roosevelt, the 26th Leader of the US, assumed an essential part in extending the country's protection endeavors. Roosevelt, profoundly affected by the works of Muir, regulated the making of the US Woods Administration in 1905 and laid out various public parks and landmarks during his administration. His obligation to protection set a trend for future pioneers and highlighted the significance of offsetting monetary improvement with ecological conservation.

Protection in the Mid twentieth Hundred years:

The mid twentieth century saw the rise of coordinated preservation developments with a more extensive degree and a more worldwide point of view. Worries about asset exhaustion, natural life protection, and the effect of industrialization on the climate became focal subjects.

Aldo Leopold, frequently viewed as the dad of natural life environment, underscored the requirement for a land ethic that recognized the interconnectedness of every single living thing. In his powerful book, "A Sand District Chronicle," distributed post mortem in 1949, Leopold pushed for a moral system that stretched out past human interests to envelop the prosperity of the whole environment.

Rachel Carson, a sea life scholar, and creator, pointed out the unfavorable impacts of pesticides, especially DDT, in her fundamental work "Quiet Spring," distributed in 1962. Carson's book ignited far and wide worry about the ecological effects of manufactured synthetic substances and is frequently credited with catalyzing the cutting edge natural development.

The Ecological Development:

The mid-twentieth century saw the ascent of the ecological development, a more extensive and all the more politically charged emphasis of preservation endeavors. This development, filled by worries about contamination, overpopulation, and the outcomes of industrialization, picked up speed following occasions, for example, the Cuyahoga Waterway bursting into flames in 1969 and the St Nick Barbara oil slick in 1969.

Earth Day, first saw on April 22, 1970, denoted a urgent second in the ecological development. A large number of individuals across the US partook in meetings, shows, and instructive occasions, requesting more prominent ecological securities.

The progress of Earth Day added to the foundation of the Ecological Assurance Organization (EPA) soon thereafter and the entry of key natural regulation, including the Spotless Air Act and the Perfect Water Act.

Worldwide Preservation Endeavors:

As consciousness of worldwide natural issues developed, global preservation endeavors turned out to be progressively unmistakable. The Unified Countries Gathering on the Human Climate, held in Stockholm in 1972, denoted the principal significant worldwide meeting on ecological issues. The gathering brought about the foundation of the Unified Countries Climate Program (UNEP) and laid the preparation for future worldwide ecological arrangements.

One of the main global preservation arrangements is the Show on Organic Variety (CBD), embraced in 1992 during the Earth Culmination in Rio de Janeiro. The CBD intends to monitor organic variety, guarantee the practical utilization of regular assets, and advance the fair and evenhanded sharing of advantages emerging from hereditary assets.

Difficulties and Debates:

While preservation endeavors have accomplished critical victories, they have additionally confronted difficulties and discussions. The strain between financial turn of events and ecological conservation stays a focal issue, especially in emerging countries where the quest for monetary development can in some cases come to the detriment of environments and biodiversity.

The idea of "post preservation," which includes making safeguarded regions and barring neighborhood networks, has been censured for its possible pessimistic effect on native people groups and nearby livelihoods. Finding some kind of harmony between preservation objectives and the necessities of neighborhood networks stays a perplexing and continuous test.

One more area of dispute is the job of innovation in protection. While propels in innovation have given important apparatuses to checking and overseeing biological systems, discusses endure about the morals of mediations like hereditary designing and de-eradication endeavors.

The Anthropocene and New Protection Ideal models:

The Anthropocene, a term used to depict the ongoing geographical age set apart by huge human effect on the World's geography and biological systems, has prodded a reconsideration of protection standards. Perceiving that people are currently a prevailing power forming the planet, progressives are investigating new methodologies that incorporate human requirements with natural supportability.

One such change in perspective is the idea of "rewilding," which includes reestablishing environments to their regular state by once again introducing local species and permitting normal cycles to occur. The renewed introduction of wolves to Yellowstone Public Park in the US is an eminent illustration of effective rewilding endeavors.

Protection in the 21st 100 years:

In the 21st hundred years, preservation endeavors keep on developing in light of arising ecological difficulties, including environmental change, territory misfortune, and the deficiency of biodiversity. The criticalness of resolving these issues has prompted expanded coordinated effort between researchers, policymakers, non-administrative associations (NGOs), and neighborhood networks.

Progresses in innovation, like satellite symbolism, DNA examination, and AI, are giving new devices to observing and overseeing biological systems. Progressives are additionally investigating creative supporting instruments, for example, installments for biological system administrations and effect financial planning, to subsidize preservation drives.

Local area based protection, which includes enabling neighborhood networks to effectively take part in and benefit from preservation endeavors, has acquired noticeable quality. This approach perceives the significance of drawing in and affecting nearby individuals in dynamic cycles and underlines the interconnectedness of human prosperity and ecological wellbeing.

1.2 Emergence and Evolution of Zebra Warriors

In the core of the African savannah, where the sun paints the sky with tints of orange and the breeze conveys the beat of the untamed wild, a special local area known as the Zebra Fighters arose. The tale of the Zebra Champions is one woven with strings of social extravagance, flexibility, and a profound association with the land they call home. As we dig into the rise and development of the Zebra Fighters, we uncover a story that rises above time, formed by the recurring pattern of the regular world and the soul of still up in the air to explore the difficulties of their current circumstance.

Antiquated Roots and Social Establishment

The foundations of the Zebra Champions stretch back through the hallways of time, tracking down sustenance in the old customs of the native networks that occupied the African savannah. These people group, profoundly receptive to the rhythms of nature, noticed the zebras - the superb high contrast striped equines that meandered the tremendous scenes. As far as they might be concerned, the zebras were not simply creatures; they were images of solidarity, solidarity, and the agreeable concurrence of different components.

The social underpinning of the Zebra Fighters lies in a significant respect for the land and its occupants. The zebras, with their particular stripes, became significant of the interconnectedness of every living thing. These antiquated networks, in their insight, perceived the significance of variety and the job it played in the endurance of the system.

Customs and Customs

The rise of the Zebra Fighters was set apart by intricate ceremonies and customs that tried to lay out a profound association with the zebras and the regular world. These customs were not simple services; they were significant articulations of the local area's ethos and an affirmation of the powers that represented their reality.

One such custom was the Dance of Stripes, a stylized exhibition that reflected the elegant developments of zebras across the savannah. Through multifaceted movement, the heroes looked to exemplify the solidarity, flexibility, and variety represented by the stripes of the zebras. The Dance of Stripes turned into a mutual festival, a representative demonstration of lining up with the normal request of the world.

The Social occasion of the Group was another vital custom, uniting the local area to share stories, astuteness, and encounters. Like the zebras shaping defensive circles around their young, the Get-together of the Crowd supported the significance of fortitude and aggregate strength despite challenges.

Flexibility Even with Affliction

As the networks developed, so did the job of the Zebra Heroes. The cruel real factors of the African savannah, with its unusual environments and constant dangers, requested a reaction that rose above the person. The champions needed to adjust to make due, reflecting the zebras that explored the consistently moving scenes with beauty and flexibility.

Versatility turned into a foundation of the Zebra Fighters' personality. They figured out how to peruse the indications of nature, predict changes in atmospheric conditions, and expect the developments of hunters. This flexibility was not only an endurance system; it was an impression of the significant association the fighters kept up with the climate.

Development of the Zebra Hero Code

Key to the development of the Zebra Champions was the codification of their standards and values. The Zebra Champion Code, a bunch of core values roused by the stripes of the zebras, turned into the ethical compass for the local area. It embodied the quintessence of solidarity, flexibility, and variety that characterized the heroes.

The primary stripe of the code accentuated solidarity - the comprehension that strength lies in fellowship.

Similarly as zebras structure a defensive circle around their young, the Zebra Fighters perceived the force of aggregate fortitude in exploring the difficulties of life on the savannah.

The subsequent stripe highlighted versatility - the capacity to flourish despite change. Similar as the zebras that advanced to make due in different conditions, the champions embraced change as an innate piece of their excursion. They figured out how to adjust their systems, methods, and ways of life to the consistently moving elements of the savannah.

The third stripe celebrated variety - the acknowledgment that every individual brought a novel arrangement of abilities and points of view to the local area. The fighters comprehended that it was the mosaic of qualities, woven together like the stripes of zebras, that invigorated their aggregate soul.

Initiative and the Ancestral Chamber

As the Zebra Fighters kept on developing, an arrangement of initiative arose to direct the local area through the intricacies of their reality. The Ancestral Committee, made out of regarded elderly folks and experienced champions, turned into the foundation of independent direction and compromise. The gathering drew motivation from the libertarian structure saw in zebra crowds, where every part assumes an imperative part.

Initiative in the Zebra Heroes was not about predominance but rather about shrewdness, experience, and a profound comprehension of the land. The ancestral pioneers were picked for their capacity to decipher the indications of nature, their obligation to the Zebra Hero Code, and their ability to cultivate solidarity inside the local area.

Difficulties and Wins

The excursion of the Zebra Fighters was not without its difficulties. The consistently present danger of hunters, the brutal components of the savannah, and the need to get assets for the local area tried the fighters' determination. Nonetheless, it was exactly these difficulties that turned into the cauldron for the fashioning of their versatility and assurance.

Wins for the Zebra Champions frequently came as mutual accomplishments. Effectively battling off outside dangers, concocting creative techniques for asset the board, and developing manageable practices that lined up with the climate were all demonstration of the adequacy of the Zebra Champion lifestyle.

The Tradition of the Zebra Heroes

As time spread out across the African savannah, the tradition of the Zebra Heroes became imbued in the actual texture of the land. Their story was gone down through ages, turning into a living demonstration of the getting through force of solidarity, versatility, and variety.

The Zebra Champions made a permanent imprint on the social legacy of the district. Their moves, ceremonies, and the Zebra Champion Code became customs as well as core values for ensuing ages. The insight of the elderly folks, the flexibility of the champions, and the veneration for the climate framed the foundation of a heritage that reverberated through the ages

1.3 Founding Principles and Objectives

The establishing standards and targets of any association, development, or local area lay the basis for its personality, reason, and direction. These core values act as the ethical compass, forming direction, affecting way of behaving, and characterizing the general mission. Whether with regards to a country, a not-for-profit association, a social development, or a business substance, an unmistakable comprehension of establishing standards and targets is vital to laying out a practical and intentional system. In this investigation, we dive into the meaning of these basic components, analyzing their part in forming establishments and developments across different areas.

Characterizing Establishing Standards:

At the core of any aggregate undertaking lies a bunch of rules that eloquent the guiding principle, convictions, and central insights that support its presence. Establishing standards act as the philosophical establishment whereupon a substance or development is fabricated, giving a cognizant system to direction and conduct. These standards frequently epitomize the goals and yearnings of the originators, forming the association's way of life and affecting its connections with the outer world.

For a country, establishing standards might be cherished in protected reports, illustrating the privileges, obligations, and goals that characterize the aggregate personality. In a business setting, establishing standards could appear as a statement of purpose, articulating the organization's fundamental beliefs, vision, and obligation to partners. Social developments, as well, are in many cases established in establishing rules that expressive the ideal change, the qualities directing the development, and the vision for a superior future.

Verifiable Points of view on Establishing Standards:

Since the beginning of time, the foundation of countries, organizations, and developments has been joined by a cognizant enunciation of establishing standards.

The American Unrest, for example, led to the US with its Statement of Freedom, a record that cherishes the standards of freedom, correspondence, and the quest for joy. The French Unrest correspondingly saw the announcement of the Statement of the Freedoms of Man and of the Resident, accentuating standards of common liberties and political portrayal.

In the domain of business, famous organizations frequently follow their prosperity back to a bunch of establishing rules that directed their initial choices. For example,

Google's obligation to coordinating the world's data and making it generally open and helpful mirrors the organization's establishing standards, which focus on development, client centricity, and a worldwide viewpoint.

Social developments, as well, are moved by establishing rules that expressive the complaints, desires, and upsides of individuals included. The Social liberties Development in the US, for instance, was grounded in standards of uniformity, equity, and the destruction of racial separation.

The Job of Establishing Goals:

While establishing standards articulate the fundamental qualities and convictions, establishing targets give a guide to activity, characterizing the particular objectives and achievements an element or development looks to accomplish. Goals act as the substantial articulations of standards, making an interpretation of conceptual beliefs into quantifiable results. Whether as regulative objectives for a country, execution focuses for a business, or achievements for a social development, establishing targets give clearness and heading.

With regards to a country, establishing goals might incorporate the foundation of a simply general set of laws, the advancement of financial thriving, or the assurance of specific privileges and opportunities to residents. Organizations, then again, frequently articulate establishing goals connected with piece of the pie, benefit, or social and ecological effect. Social developments set goals that line up with their standards, like authoritative changes, cultural changes in mentalities, or the destroying of unfair practices.

Establishing Standards and Targets in Country Building:

The foundation of a country is a perplexing and diverse cycle that requires a reasonable explanation of establishing standards and targets. Countries are not simply topographical substances but rather friendly builds based on shared values, verifiable accounts, and yearnings for what's in store. Establishing standards with regards to country assembling frequently track down articulation in sacred archives, sanctions, or statements that lay the basis for the country's personality.

The US, for instance, is established on standards like majority rules government, individual privileges, and the quest for bliss, as framed in the Announcement of Autonomy and the Constitution. These standards structure the reason for a bunch of goals, including the foundation of an administration that gets its power from the assent of the represented, the security of individual opportunities, and the quest for the normal government assistance.

Likewise, the post-politically-sanctioned racial segregation South Africa explained its establishing standards as Reality and Compromise Commission, stressing the upsides of truth, equity, and compromise. The goals included tending to the verifiable treacheries of politically-sanctioned racial segregation, encouraging public mending, and building a more comprehensive and evenhanded society.

Establishing Standards in Business Associations:

In the domain of business, establishing standards assume a significant part in molding the way of life, values, and key heading of an association. Organizations frequently articulate their standards through statements of purpose, sets of rules, or corporate social obligation (CSR) drives. These standards go past benefit making and epitomize the association's more extensive commitments to society, ecological manageability, and the prosperity of partners.

The worldwide organization Patagonia, for example, has fabricated its character around natural manageability and social obligation. Its statement of purpose mirrors a promise to "construct the best item, inflict damage, use business to move and execute answers for the ecological emergency." The establishing standards, established in natural stewardship and moral strategic policies, guide the organization's targets, including the decrease of its natural impression and backing for grassroots ecological drives.

Also, the innovation monster Apple is directed by standards of development, plan greatness, and client experience. These standards are converted into goals like the formation of state of the art items, a consistent UI, and a promise to ecological maintainability.

Establishing Targets and Social Developments:

Social developments, driven by the longing for cultural change, frequently articulate their establishing standards through pronouncements, announcements, or mission statements. These standards give a moral and philosophical starting point for the development's goals, which are the substantial results the development looks to accomplish. Whether tending to social liberties, orientation fairness, ecological equity, or other cultural issues, social developments outline their targets inside the more extensive setting of their core values.

The women's activist development, for instance, is grounded in standards of orientation fairness, strengthening, and the destroying of man centric designs. Goals of the women's activist development incorporate lawful changes, changes in cultural mentalities, and the advancement of equivalent open doors for all sexual orientations.

The natural development, incorporating different gatherings and causes, is directed by standards of biological maintainability, protection, and environment equity. Goals of the natural development frequently incorporate strategy changes, corporate obligation, and public mindfulness missions to resolve squeezing ecological issues.

Establishing Standards and Goals in Philanthropic Associations:

Not-for-profit associations, driven by a mission to resolve social issues, are based after establishing standards and goals that line up with their vision for positive change. These associations, frequently alluded to as NGOs (non-legislative associations) or magnanimous associations, articulate their standards in statements of purpose, directing their goals and exercises to satisfy their cultural reason.

Specialists Without Lines (Médecins Sans Frontières), a clinical philanthropic association, is directed by standards of clinical morals, fairness, and the arrangement of clinical consideration to those out of luck. Its targets incorporate conveying crisis clinical consideration, pushing for the freedoms of minimized populaces, and answering wellbeing emergencies all around the world.

Pardon Worldwide, a worldwide basic liberties association, is established in standards of equity, balance, and the security of common freedoms. Its goals incorporate upholding for the arrival of detainees of still, small voice, considering states responsible for denials of basic freedoms, and elevating global collaboration to address fundamental shameful acts.

Variation and Advancement of Establishing Standards and Targets:

The versatility and advancement of establishing standards and targets are fundamental for the supported significance and outcome of countries, associations, developments, and organizations. As cultural standards change, outer conditions shift, and new difficulties arise, the capacity to reevaluate and, if important, rethink these essential components becomes basic.

Countries, for example, may have to return to their establishing standards and goals to address developing thoughts of citizenship, civil rights, and natural maintainability. Established revisions, authoritative changes, or cultural exchanges might be started to guarantee that the country's central standards stay intelligent of the aggregate qualities and goals of its residents.

Business associations, working in unique business sectors, should persistently reconsider their establishing standards and goals to stay cutthroat and socially dependable. This might include acclimations to plans of action, item contributions, or manageability practices to line up with changing customer assumptions, administrative scenes, or mechanical progressions.

Social developments, while established in getting through standards, may have to adjust their targets to answer moving cultural elements. The LGBTQ+ privileges development, for instance, has advanced its goals from tying down fundamental social liberties to supporting for more extensive cultural acknowledgment and acknowledgment of assorted orientation personalities and sexual directions.

Philanthropic associations, especially those tending to worldwide difficulties, should stay deft in their methodology. The developing idea of issues, for example, environmental change, neediness, or medical care requires a ceaseless reassessment of establishing standards and targets to guarantee compelling reactions to arising difficulties.

Challenges in Maintaining Establishing Standards and Targets:

While the explanation of establishing standards and goals gives a reasonable structure, this present reality execution and protection of these beliefs frequently present difficulties. Inside and outside pressures, contending interests, and unanticipated conditions can present deterrents to the acknowledgment of an element's core values and goals.

With regards to countries, political polarization, financial disparities, and social variety can make pressures that challenge the all inclusiveness of establishing standards. Offsetting individual opportunities with cultural prosperity, guaranteeing equivalent open doors for assorted networks, and exploring international intricacies are continuous difficulties for countries focused on maintaining their fundamental standards.

Business associations might confront difficulties in accommodating benefit thought processes with socially mindful practices. Tensions to boost investor esteem, financial vulnerabilities, and moral problems in supply chains can test an organization's obligation to its establishing standards. Finding some kind of harmony between monetary achievement and moral direct requires steady watchfulness and versatility.

Social developments, notwithstanding their principled establishments, can experience inward divisions, philosophical movements, and outer resistance that challenge their goals. Keeping up with solidarity inside different developments, tending to multifaceted issues, and answering counter-developments require vital route to really propel their establishing standards.

Not-for-profit associations, dependent on subsidizing sources and dependent upon administrative conditions, may confront provokes in remaining consistent with their central goal while adjusting to evolving conditions. Offsetting monetary maintainability with social effect, tending to giver assumptions, and answering advancing local area needs are continuous contemplations for these associations.

Establishing Standards and Targets in the Advanced Age:

In the contemporary time, the advanced age has acquainted new aspects with the explanation and acknowledgment of establishing standards and goals. Quick progressions in innovation, the interconnectedness of worldwide frameworks, and the democratization of data present the two valuable open doors and difficulties for substances exploring the computerized scene.

Countries wrestle with issues of computerized power, digital dangers, and the moral ramifications of arising advancements. The standards of security, opportunity of articulation, and admittance to data take on new importance in the computerized age. Goals might incorporate the improvement of strong network protection gauges, the foundation of moral structures for man-made brainpower, and the advancement of computerized proficiency.

Business associations, working in an undeniably digitalized economy, face objectives connected with information protection, online security, and dependable utilization of innovation. Establishing standards might stretch out to responsibilities to natural manageability in server farms, moral practices in information examination, and the reception of comprehensive advancements. Goals might include utilizing innovation for advancement, extending computerized benefits, and tending to the computerized partition.

Social developments outfit the force of computerized stages to intensify their messages, activate backing, and impact change. Standards of online activism, advanced freedoms, and data openness shape the targets of developments in the computerized age. Targets might incorporate utilizing virtual entertainment for support, countering on the web disinformation, and advancing computerized inclusivity.

Philanthropic associations, embracing advanced apparatuses for raising support, correspondence, and program conveyance, wrestle with moral contemplations connected with information use and online commitment. Standards of straightforwardness, advanced value, and mindful tech reception guide their targets. Goals might include utilizing innovation for social effect, extending computerized admittance for under-estimated networks, and guaranteeing moral utilization of information.

Establishing Standards and Goals in the Worldwide Setting:

In a time of globalization, the interconnectivity of countries, organizations, social developments, and charitable associations has expansive ramifications for the explanation and acknowledgment of establishing standards and targets. Worldwide difficulties, for example, environmental change, pandemics, and financial disparities highlight the requirement for cooperative and transnational ways to deal with address shared concerns.

Countries, perceiving the worldwide effect of their activities, may adjust their establishing standards to global standards, arrangements, and supportable advancement objectives. Goals might incorporate partaking in worldwide endeavors to address environmental change, advancing common liberties universally, and adding to global harmony and security.

Global enterprises, working across borders, explore complex moral and administrative scenes. Establishing standards connected with corporate social obligation, moral stock chains, and worldwide cooperation illuminate goals, for example, advancing variety and consideration in the labor force, decreasing carbon impressions universally, and supporting economical improvement drives.

Worldwide social developments, worked with by advanced availability, encourage diverse fortitude and mindfulness. Establishing standards of worldwide equity, social inclusivity, and basic freedoms shape targets that rise above public limits. Goals might include worldwide backing, coordinated effort with worldwide accomplices, and resolving issues with worldwide ramifications, for example, outcast emergencies or general wellbeing crises.

Worldwide not-for-profit associations, tending to worldwide difficulties, should fit their standards with the different social settings in which they work. Establishing standards connected with social awareness, worldwide inclusivity, and practical improvement guide goals, for example, advancing instructive value universally, answering helpful emergencies, and cultivating diverse comprehension.

Chapter 2

Zebra Warriors in Action

The sun plunges low not too far off, creating long shaded areas across the African savannah. In this tremendous and dynamic scene, the Zebra Champions show signs of life, typifying the soul of flexibility, solidarity, and versatility. As we dive into the activities of the Zebra Champions, we investigate how this interesting local area explores difficulties, cultivates solidarity inside its positions, and jelly the old practices that have characterized its personality for ages.

Adjusting to the Rhythms of Nature:

The existence of the Zebra Heroes is unpredictably woven into the texture of the regular world. From the changing seasons to the movements of prey and hunters, the heroes are skilled at perusing the inconspicuous signs that oversee the rhythms of the savannah. This capacity to adjust to the recurring pattern of nature isn't simply a step by step process for surviving yet a demonstration of the profound association the Zebra Heroes keep up with their current circumstance.

When confronted with the difficulties of eccentric weather conditions or moving scenes, the Zebra Heroes show a wonderful ability to change their procedures. Whether it includes adjusting relocation courses to track down water or expecting the developments of hunters, the fighters consistently coordinate into the powerful embroidery of the savannah. This versatility, established in a comprehension of the interconnectedness of every living thing, permits the Zebra Fighters to flourish even despite affliction.

Safeguarding the Crowd:

Key to the ethos of the Zebra Champions is the guideline of solidarity and aggregate strength. The fighters comprehend that their endurance is inherently connected to the prosperity of the whole local area. Similar as the defensive circles shaped by zebras around their young, the Zebra Champions go about as gatekeepers of the group, guaranteeing the wellbeing and success of the whole crowd.

At the point when outer dangers loom, for example, the presence of hunters or the difficulties presented by ecological changes, the Zebra Champions rally together to frame an impressive protection. Through facilitated endeavors and a common obligation to the Zebra Hero Code, they fight off difficulties that would be unconquerable for people acting alone. This aggregate flexibility not just shields the quick prosperity of the local area yet additionally builds up the bonds that characterize the Zebra Fighters.

Saving Social Practices:

The customs of the Zebra Heroes are not relics of the past; they are living articulations of a social legacy went down through ages. Customs, functions, and moves assume a pivotal part in safeguarding the character of the Zebra Fighters and supporting their association with the land. These social practices act as a wellspring of solidarity, flexibility, and a common feeling of direction.

The Dance of Stripes, a stately presentation that reflects the developments of zebras across the savannah, isn't simply an exhibition; it is a representative demonstration of reaffirming the solidarity and variety that characterize the Zebra Fighter people group. The Get-together of the Crowd, where stories are shared, shrewdness is passed down, and bonds are reinforced, is a demonstration of the significance of public ties notwithstanding difficulties.

The Zebra Fighters comprehend that the protection of social customs is certainly not a static undertaking however a unique cycle that develops with the times. While regarding the antiquated practices that characterize their personality, they additionally integrate new components that reverberate with the contemporary difficulties they face. This versatile methodology guarantees that the social tradition of the Zebra Fighters stays pertinent and dynamic.

Inventive Ways to deal with Asset The executives:

Endurance on the savannah requires a sharp comprehension of asset the board, and the Zebra Fighters approach this test with development and premonition. Perceiving the sensitive harmony between human necessities and the soundness of the biological system, the fighters utilize manageable practices that guarantee the life span of imperative assets.

In the midst of shortage, the Zebra Fighters exhibit a significant regard for the land by executing rotational brushing designs, permitting vegetation to recover and guaranteeing the prosperity of both untamed life and the local area. They perceive that overexploitation of assets risks their own endurance as well as the multifaceted snare of life that supports the whole savannah biological system.

The Zebra Champions' obligation to supportable asset the executives stretches out past prompt necessities, incorporating a comprehensive comprehension of their job as stewards of the land. By mixing customary environmental information with creative methodologies, they set a model for agreeable conjunction with nature, cultivating a model that offsets human exercises with the safeguarding of biodiversity.

Instruction and Passing Down Insight:

The transmission of information is a foundation of the Zebra Champion people group. Seniors, venerated for their insight and experience, assume a urgent part in teaching the more youthful ages.

This intergenerational trade guarantees the coherence of social practices, abilities to survive, and the core values embodied in the Zebra Fighter Code.

Youthful heroes go through an exhaustive instruction that goes past conventional abilities to incorporate a profound comprehension of the interconnectedness of the savannah's environments. They learn not just how to explore the actual difficulties of their current circumstance yet additionally the significance of moral direct, administration, and solidarity despite difficulty.

The instructive acts of the Zebra Fighters feature the worth they put on all encompassing turn of events, perceiving that a balanced champion is better prepared to add to the local area's versatility and manageability. This obligation to training mirrors a forward-looking point of view that recognizes the switching elements of the world up them.

Confronting Outside Tensions with Tact:

In the consistently changing scene of the savannah, the Zebra Champions once in a while end up communicating with outer powers — be it adjoining networks, changing environment designs, or the infringement of advancement. In such examples, the fighters utilize a political methodology, looking to encourage understanding and participation as opposed to depending on struggle.

Understanding that the interconnectedness of the savannah reaches out past their nearby local area, the Zebra Heroes take part in discourse with adjoining clans and networks. These associations are directed by standards of common regard, shared asset the executives, and the acknowledgment of each gathering's exceptional social legacy. By fashioning collusions and coordinated efforts, the Zebra Fighters explore outer tensions while saving the respectability of their local area.

Furthermore, the Zebra Champions effectively draw in with outside substances, including preservation associations and legislative bodies, to advocate for supportable practices and the security of the savannah's biodiversity. Their conciliatory endeavors stretch out past quick worries, mirroring a guarantee to the more extensive prosperity of the whole environment.

Utilizing Innovation for Protection:

Perceiving the force of development, the Zebra Fighters have embraced innovation as an instrument for preservation. While established in old customs, they influence current progressions to screen ecological changes, track natural life relocations, and speak with adjoining networks. Satellite symbolism, GPS innovation, and cell phones become necessary parts of their protection tool stash.

Through the essential utilization of innovation, the Zebra Fighters upgrade their capacity to safeguard the savannah and its occupants. Drones are utilized to screen enormous regions, identify expected dangers, and accumulate information on untamed life populaces. This combination of innovation into their preservation endeavors mirrors a practical methodology that recognizes the advantages of current devices in protecting old scenes.

The Zebra Fighters' usage of innovation isn't a takeoff from their social roots however a show of their versatile mentality. By embracing advancement, they guarantee that their protection rehearses stay powerful and economical notwithstanding developing difficulties.

Tending to Environmental Change with Strength:

The effect of environmental change resonates across the African savannah, presenting difficulties to both natural life and human networks. The Zebra Fighters, personally associated with the rhythms of the land, face the truth of changing environment designs with a mix of strength and proactive measures.

Noticing shifts in atmospheric conditions, the Zebra Fighters have changed their movement courses and asset the executives methodologies. By grasping the interconnectedness of environment, vegetation, and untamed life, they adjust their way of life to limit natural effect while guaranteeing the maintainability of their local area.

In tending to environmental change, the Zebra Fighters effectively partake in local and worldwide drives pointed toward relieving its belongings. Their commitment goes past endurance; it mirrors a pledge to the more extensive ecological local area and an acknowledgment of their obligation as stewards of the savannah.

Local area Based Preservation and The travel industry:

The Zebra Fighters perceive the capability of mindful the travel industry as a way to support their local area as well as advance preservation. By opening their territories to eco-accommodating the travel industry, they share their social legacy, conventional information, and the magnificence of the savannah with guests from around the world.

This people group based preservation approach guarantees that travel industry helps the Zebra Champion people group straightforwardly, giving financial open doors and cultivating a more profound comprehension of the cooperative connection among people and nature. Guests are not detached eyewitnesses but rather dynamic members in the protection endeavors of the Zebra Heroes.

The travel industry income is reinvested in local area advancement tasks, schooling, and ecological security drives. This manageable model of the travel industry lines up with the Zebra Heroes' obligation to protecting their social legacy while adding to the worldwide discussion on preservation.

Difficulties and Future Possibilities:

While the Zebra Champions have shown momentous strength and flexibility, they are not resistant to the difficulties that persevere in the advanced world. Outside pressures, financial vulnerabilities, and the proceeded with effect of environmental change present continuous difficulties to the maintainability of their lifestyle.

Protecting social customs despite globalization and quick cultural changes requires vital reasoning and a proactive methodology. The Zebra Champions should figure out some kind of harmony between embracing components of innovation that line up with their qualities and protecting the antiquated practices that characterize their personality.

Environmental change, with its flighty weather conditions and natural movements, requires progressing transformation procedures. The Zebra Heroes might have to persistently reconsider their asset the board rehearses, movement examples, and preservation endeavors to guarantee the drawn out practicality of their local area.

Monetary supportability, while upheld by local area based the travel industry, requires cautious thought of the likely effect on the climate and the fragile equilibrium of the savannah environment. Finding some kind of harmony between financial turn of events and ecological preservation is a nuanced challenge that the Zebra Champions explore with a pledge to capable practices.

The Zebra Fighters likewise face the test of outside substances looking to take advantage of the assets of the savannah for financial increase. Preservation endeavors should remember backing and joint effort for a more extensive scale to safeguard the Zebra Hero people group as well as the whole environment they occupy.

As they explore these difficulties, the Zebra Champions stay an image of flexibility, solidarity, and social pride. Their story offers bits of knowledge into maintainable living, the agreeable concurrence of people and nature, and the significance of adjusting old customs to satisfy the needs of the cutting edge world.

1. **Protecting Endangered Species**
   Safeguarding imperiled species is a basic for keeping up with the planet's biodiversity and biological equilibrium. As different species face dangers, for example, environment misfortune, environmental change, and poaching, coordinated endeavors are expected to forestall their eradication. Preservation drives center around saving natural surroundings, carrying out economical practices, and battling unlawful exchange.

   Safeguarding regular natural surroundings guarantees that jeopardized species have reasonable conditions for reproducing, taking care of, and flourishing. Moreover, drives to address environmental change assume a significant part, as movements in weather conditions and temperatures can unfavorably influence biological systems, upsetting the fragile equilibrium fundamental for some species' endurance.

   Against poaching measures and severe regulations battle the unlawful exchange of jeopardized species and their body parts. Public mindfulness and schooling efforts are significant in encouraging a feeling of obligation and gathering support for protection endeavors.

   At last, shielding jeopardized species isn't simply an ecological concern; it is an aggregate liability to safeguard the perplexing snare of life that supports our planet. Protection endeavors benefit jeopardized species as well as add to the general wellbeing and strength of environments, guaranteeing a more economical and agreeable concurrence among people and the regular world.

2. Habitat Restoration Initiatives

Notwithstanding raising natural difficulties, territory reclamation drives have arisen as essential undertakings pointed toward resuscitating and safeguarding environments around the world. These drives perceive the interconnectedness of every living thing and the crucial job solid natural surroundings play in supporting biodiversity, managing environment, and giving fundamental biological system administrations. Natural surroundings rebuilding isn't simply a reaction to ecological corruption; it is a proactive procedure to address the main drivers of environment misfortune and advance long haul biological flexibility.

Vital to territory reclamation is the revival of corrupted or annihilated biological systems, going from backwoods and wetlands to meadows and coral reefs. One eminent model is the rebuilding of debased woodlands, where endeavors include tree planting, obtrusive species expulsion, and cultivating normal recovery processes. By recharging vegetation, these drives add to carbon sequestration, improve water quality, and give natural surroundings to a different cluster of animal categories.

Wetlands, indispensable for water filtration and flood control, additionally benefit from reclamation drives. Endeavors incorporate reestablishing regular hydrological processes, controlling intrusive species, and making cushion zones. The reclamation of wetlands shields against flooding as well as improves water quality and gives essential favorable places to different sea-going species.

Likewise, prairie reclamation drives center around fighting desertification, forestalling soil disintegration, and advancing the recuperation of local plant species. These endeavors add to keeping up with biodiversity, supporting nibbling creatures, and safeguarding the sensitive equilibrium of field biological systems.

Submerged environments face one of a kind difficulties, with coral reefs experiencing dying, contamination, and living space obliteration. Coral reef reclamation projects include methods, for example, coral transplantation, fake reef designs, and marine safeguarded regions. These drives mean to modify the flexibility of coral reefs, guaranteeing their capacity to help marine life and shield shores from storm floods.

Effective natural surroundings rebuilding requires a multi-faceted methodology, incorporating biological contemplations as well as drawing in neighborhood networks, policymakers, and organizations. Cooperation between states, non-legislative associations, and nearby networks is vital for address the intricate drivers of natural surroundings debasement, including deforestation, contamination, and impractical land use rehearses.

Additionally, living space reclamation drives frequently incorporate logical exploration, observing, and versatile administration methodologies to survey the adequacy of rebuilding strategies and refine approaches over the long haul. This iterative cycle guarantees that rebuilding endeavors line up with natural standards and add to the drawn out strength of biological systems.

Schooling and public mindfulness assume an imperative part in the progress of environment rebuilding drives. Conveying the significance of biological systems, the worth of biodiversity, and the unmistakable advantages of rebuilding cultivates a feeling of obligation and supports local area contribution. Including neighborhood networks in rebuilding exercises upgrades the viability of drives as well as makes a feeling of stewardship, guaranteeing the supported consideration of reestablished living spaces.

As the worldwide local area wrestles with squeezing ecological difficulties, natural surroundings rebuilding drives stand as encouraging signs for a more maintainable future. By perceiving the inborn worth of solid environments and effectively attempting to invert natural surroundings debasement, these drives add to the conservation of biodiversity, environment guideline, and the general prosperity of the planet. The outcome of environment reclamation isn't simply estimated in that frame of mind of scenes; it is a demonstration of mankind's obligation to coinciding agreeably with the regular world.

3. **Community-Based Conservation Programs**

In the domain of protection, local area based programs have arisen as strong instruments chasing after manageable ecological practices. These drives perceive the crucial job nearby networks play in saving biodiversity, supporting biological systems, and cultivating an amicable connection among people and the normal world. Local area based protection rises above conventional hierarchical methodologies, setting neighborhood inhabitants at the front of natural stewardship. This cooperative model tends to environmental difficulties as well as advances social value, financial turn of events, and social safeguarding.

The Substance of Local area Based Preservation:

At its center, local area based preservation underscores the dynamic cooperation and commitment of nearby networks in the administration and assurance of regular assets. Not at all like customary protection models that might distance or dislodge neighborhood populaces, local area based approaches coordinate the information, customs, and desires of local area individuals into the dynamic cycle. This guarantees that preservation techniques are logically important, maintainable, and aware of neighborhood customs.

Engaging Nearby People group:

A major part of local area based preservation is engaging neighborhood networks to take responsibility for endeavors. By including occupants in arranging, execution, and observing cycles, these projects encourage a feeling of obligation and stewardship. Engaged people group are bound to take on feasible practices, effectively partake in untamed life assurance, and champion the protection of their normal environmental elements.

Connecting Protection and Livelihoods:

Local area based protection programs perceive the perplexing connection between natural wellbeing and local area occupations. Feasible asset the executives rehearses are incorporated with monetary open doors that benefit neighborhood inhabitants. For example, eco-the travel industry drives, supportable farming practices, and mindful gathering of woodland items can give roads to pay age while at the same time advancing protection objectives.

In Namibia, the Local area Based Normal Asset The executives (CBNRM) program represents this methodology. Nearby people group are allowed the freedoms to oversee and profit from untamed life assets. This has prompted the foundation of collective conservancies, where networks participate in ecotourism, profiting from the financial returns while effectively shielding untamed life populaces.

Social Safeguarding and Native Information:

Local area based protection perceives the characteristic worth of native information and social practices in keeping up with natural equilibrium. Native people group frequently have special bits of knowledge into the neighborhood climate, customary protection techniques, and the supportable utilization of normal assets. These projects regard and coordinate native points of view, guaranteeing that protection drives are socially delicate and lined up with conventional natural information.

In the Amazon rainforest, native networks effectively take part in local area based preservation endeavors. These drives draw on ages of collected information about supportable horticulture, therapeutic plants, and concurrence with untamed life.

By esteeming and consolidating native viewpoints, local area based preservation programs improve their viability and cultivate a more profound association among individuals and their current circumstance.

Training and Mindfulness:

An essential part of local area based protection is the advancement of natural training and mindfulness. By encouraging a more profound comprehension of the interconnectedness of biological systems and the worth of biodiversity, these projects engage networks to settle on informed conclusions about regular asset the executives. Schooling drives might incorporate studios, preparing projects, and local area outreach endeavors pointed toward imparting a feeling of ecological stewardship.

In Madagascar, where remarkable and jeopardized species are found, local area based preservation programs team up with nearby schools and local area pioneers to teach occupants about the significance of safeguarding their particular environments. This grassroots methodology improves protection mindfulness as well as develops a culture of ecological obligation among the more youthful age.

Local area Based Marine Protection:

Seaside people group are frequently at the front of marine preservation endeavors, perceiving the basic job seas play in supporting life. Local area based marine preservation includes nearby occupants in the assurance of marine environments, the requirement of fishing guidelines, and the reclamation of beach front living spaces.

In the Philippines, drives like the Tubbataha Reefs Regular Park include neighborhood networks in the administration of marine safeguarded regions. Fishers are urged to embrace feasible fishing practices, and local area individuals effectively partake in coral reef observing and rebuilding endeavors. The outcome of such projects is established in the cooperation between preservation associations and the networks that rely upon marine assets for their vocations.

Difficulties and Victories:

While people group based protection programs have shown noteworthy triumphs, they likewise face difficulties. Offsetting protection objectives with the financial necessities of neighborhood networks, tending to control elements, and exploring outside pressures are perplexing undertakings. Guaranteeing that advantages from preservation drives are fairly conveyed inside networks is fundamental for long haul achievement.

One outstanding example of overcoming adversity is the situation of the Snow Panther Confidence in Focal Asia. Local area based preservation endeavors include nearby herders in the assurance of snow panthers and their territories. Through programs like the "Snow Panther Undertaking," herders are boosted to safeguard snow panthers by getting fair pay for their part in protection.

This approach lessens human-natural life struggle as well as gives financial advantages to networks, encouraging a feeling of shared liability regarding snow panther preservation.

B. Collaborations with Local and International Entities

In a time set apart by interconnectedness and shared worldwide obligations, joint efforts among nearby and global substances have become basic for tending to complex difficulties. Whether handling ecological issues, advancing financial turn of events, or answering general wellbeing emergencies, the collaboration between nearby networks and worldwide associations makes a strong power for positive change. This cooperative methodology encourages a rich trade of information, assets, and different viewpoints, at last adding to additional thorough and practical arrangements.

Neighborhood Global Organizations in Natural Preservation:

Ecological protection is a perfect representation of a field where nearby and worldwide joint efforts yield huge effect. Nearby people group, personally associated with their environments, have important information about provincial biodiversity, reasonable asset the executives, and conventional preservation rehearses. When combined with the worldwide reach and assets of global associations, this organization makes an intense power for protecting the planet's regular legacy.

In the Amazon rainforest, associations between native networks and global preservation associations expect to safeguard biodiversity and battle deforestation. Native information adds to maintainable land-use rehearses, while worldwide substances give financing, specialized mastery, and promotion on a worldwide scale. This cooperative model protects the rainforest's one of a kind biological systems as well as maintains the freedoms and prosperity of neighborhood networks.

Financial Advancement through Neighborhood Global Joint effort:

Advancing financial improvement is one more field where coordinated efforts among neighborhood and global elements assume a groundbreaking part. Worldwide associations bring monetary assets, specialized ability, and worldwide market access, while neighborhood networks contribute their social bits of knowledge, pioneering soul, and on-the-ground understanding. This collaboration brings about drives that engage neighborhood economies, set out business open doors, and cultivate manageable turn of events.

Microfinance programs, upheld by global elements, epitomize this cooperative methodology. By giving little advances and monetary administrations to neighborhood business visionaries, these projects empower the foundation and development of independent companies. This enables networks monetarily, lessens destitution, and adds to more extensive monetary dependability.

General Wellbeing Joint efforts:

General wellbeing challenges, especially those with worldwide ramifications, request cooperative endeavors. Nearby wellbeing frameworks, frequently stressed by restricted assets, benefit from the help of worldwide associations in regions like illness anticipation, medical services foundation improvement, and crisis reaction. Cooperative drives upgrade the limit of neighborhood medical care experts, further develop admittance to fundamental administrations, and reinforce general wellbeing frameworks.

Worldwide wellbeing associations, for example, the Worldwide Asset to Battle Helps, Tuberculosis, and Jungle fever, unite nearby wellbeing specialists, global associations, and givers. This joint effort plays had an essential impact in tending to the spread of irresistible illnesses, further developing medical care framework, and propelling exploration for new therapies and immunizations.

Instruction Drives:

Instruction is a critical driver of cultural advancement, and joint efforts among nearby and worldwide elements enhance the effect of instructive drives. Worldwide associations frequently bring ability, subsidizing, and worldwide viewpoints, while nearby networks contribute social significance, logical comprehension, and grassroots associations. This cooperative methodology improves instructive access, quality, and importance, encouraging the advancement of enabled and informed social orders.

Through programs like UNESCO's Schooling for Economical Turn of events, neighborhood teachers and networks team up with global specialists to coordinate manageable practices into instructive educational plans. This drive guarantees that people in the future are furnished with the information and abilities expected to address ecological, social, and monetary difficulties.

Innovation Move and Advancement:

Coordinated efforts among nearby and worldwide elements work with the exchange of innovation and development, crossing over holes and speeding up progress. Nearby people group frequently hold one of a kind bits of knowledge into logical requirements, while global elements contribute mechanical progressions and exploration capacities. This joint effort drives comprehensive turn of events, guaranteeing that innovative arrangements are adjusted to nearby settings and add to feasible results.

In the field of environmentally friendly power, nearby global associations work with the exchange of clean energy advances to networks that need admittance to customary energy sources. By consolidating neighborhood information on energy requirements and asset accessibility with worldwide aptitude in sustainable advancements, these co-ordinated efforts advance energy autonomy, lessen natural effect, and further develop the general prosperity of networks.

Difficulties and Contemplations:

While joint efforts among neighborhood and global substances offer colossal potential, they are not without challenges. Power elements, social awarenesses, and contrasting needs can make pressures inside associations. Guaranteeing impartial investment, regarding nearby independence, and cultivating common trust are fundamental for conquering these difficulties. Furthermore, building maintainable coordinated efforts requires a drawn out responsibility, versatility, and consistent correspondence.

The potential for "parachute" or "helicopter" approaches, where outer substances force arrangements without grasping nearby settings, stays a worry. Effective joint efforts focus on co-creation, perceiving the worth of nearby information and encouraging a feeling of pride inside networks.

Adjusting the advantages of global help with the requirement for self-assurance is urgent. Engaging nearby networks to take positions of authority in cooperative endeavors guarantees that drives line up with their goals and add to practical improvement according to their own preferences.

C. Use of Technology in Conservation Efforts

Despite raising natural difficulties and biodiversity misfortune, the mix of innovation has arisen as a strong partner in protection endeavors. From satellite observing to man-made reasoning (man-made intelligence) applications, innovation assumes a critical part in social occasion information, carrying out proficient protection procedures, and connecting with networks. This marriage of development and preservation science addresses a change in outlook, upgrading our capacity to grasp, screen, and defend the regular world. In this investigation, we dig into the different ways innovation is utilized in protection, featuring its effect on biodiversity safeguarding and biological system maintainability.

1. **Remote Detecting and Satellite Innovation:**

    Satellite innovation has altered the manner in which we screen and deal with Earth's biological systems. Remote detecting devices, mounted on satellites, give an elevated perspective of scenes, empowering researchers to follow changes in vegetation, land use, and deforestation. This innovation works with continuous checking, permitting traditionalists to distinguish regions in danger and answer speedily to arising dangers.

    For example, in the Amazon rainforest, satellites are utilized to identify deforestation exercises. By breaking down changes in backwoods cover over the long run, protectionists can evaluate the effect of human exercises, track unlawful logging, and carry out measures to control deforestation. The openness of satellite information has democratized checking endeavors, enabling neighborhood networks and associations to participate in the assurance of their surroundings effectively.

2. **Man-made brainpower and AI:**

Man-made brainpower and AI calculations have become vital apparatuses in the protection tool stash. These advancements cycle tremendous measures of information, recognize designs, and produce bits of knowledge that illuminate preservation techniques. AI models can examine complex biological datasets, foresee species conveyance, and evaluate the effect of environmental change on biodiversity.

In natural life preservation, artificial intelligence fueled cameras outfitted with picture acknowledgment innovation help in the ID and following of species. These camera traps naturally dissect pictures, permitting specialists to appraise populace sizes, screen conduct, and identify possible dangers. AI calculations can likewise filter through acoustic information to recognize species in view of their vocalizations, giving a non-meddlesome strategy to observing biodiversity.

3. **Resident Science and Portable Applications:**

The ascent of portable innovation has engaged residents to take part in protection endeavors through resident science drives effectively. Versatile applications permit clients to contribute significant information, like natural life sightings, plant perceptions, and ecological circumstances. This publicly supported data upgrades the extension and size of preservation research, furnishing specialists with thorough datasets.

Stages like iNaturalist empower clients overall to archive and share perceptions of widely varied vegetation. This aggregate exertion adds to species conveyance planning, territory checking, and the disclosure of new and uncommon species. Resident science expands logical exploration as well as cultivates a feeling of natural stewardship among people, transforming them into dynamic members in protection.

4. **Preservation Robots and Automated Airborne Vehicles (UAVs):**

Preservation drones, or automated elevated vehicles (UAVs), offer a dynamic and practical way to deal with checking scenes and untamed life. Furnished with cameras, sensors, and, surprisingly, warm imaging innovation, drones give high-goal airborne information. They are especially significant in evaluating hard-to-reach or distant regions, like thick backwoods, far off islands, or regions impacted by catastrophic events.

In enemy of poaching endeavors, drones are utilized for observation and checking of safeguarded regions. They can recognize criminal operations, track poachers, and screen natural life populaces. Drones likewise assume a significant part in untamed life research, offering a non-meddlesome strategy for noticing creature conduct and gathering information on subtle species.

5. **Geographic Data Framework (GIS) Innovation:**

Geographic Data Framework (GIS) innovation is a foundation of preservation arranging and navigation. GIS incorporates spatial information, like guides and satellite symbolism, with environmental data to make complete representations of scenes. Moderates use GIS to break down natural surroundings availability, recognize basic preservation regions, and plan for the foundation of safeguarded saves.

GIS is instrumental in planning halls for natural life relocation, evaluating the effect of framework improvement on environments, and distinguishing reasonable locales for living space rebuilding. This innovation upgrades the accuracy and adequacy of protection intercessions, taking into consideration designated and proof based independent direction.

6. **Natural DNA (eDNA) Investigation:**

Natural DNA (eDNA) investigation is a state of the art innovation that changes biodiversity checking. This method includes gathering and breaking down hereditary material shed by creatures into their current circumstance, like water or soil. By separating DNA from natural examples, researchers can recognize the presence of species without direct perception.

eDNA examination is especially significant in oceanic conditions, where testing for conventional overviews might challenge. Traditionalists can distinguish the presence of uncommon or tricky species, screen changes in biodiversity, and evaluate the soundness of biological systems. This painless technique limits unsettling influence to untamed life and gives a complete comprehension of animal groups creation in a given environment.

7. **Blockchain Innovation for Preservation Straightforwardness:**

Blockchain innovation, known for its straightforwardness and security highlights, has found applications in preservation, especially in resolving issues connected with unlawful untamed life exchange and supply chains. By making unchanging and straightforward records, blockchain guarantees that data about the beginning, transportation, and offer of natural life items is detectable and unquestionable.

For instance, blockchain innovation has been utilized to follow the store network of reasonably obtained items, like lumber and fish. This guarantees that customers can pursue informed decisions, advancing moral and ecologically capable utilization. In the battle against unlawful natural life exchange, blockchain can assist with upsetting illegal organizations by making a straightforward record of exchanges.

Difficulties and Contemplations:

While the coordination of innovation in protection delivers phenomenal open doors, it isn't without challenges. The openness of innovation, the computerized partition, and the potential for unseen side-effects should be painstakingly thought of. Moreover, moral contemplations, information security, and the requirement for neighborhood local area commitment are vital in guaranteeing the mindful utilization of innovation in protection endeavors.

Moreover, the fast speed of mechanical progression expects protectionists to keep up to date with advancements and adjust their methodologies likewise. Cooperative endeavors between technologists, moderates, and neighborhood networks are fundamental to explore the intricacies and augment the advantages of mechanical arrangements.

Chapter 3

The Faces Behind Zebra Warriors

In the core of the African savannah, a local area flourishes with a soul as lively and versatile as the stripes enhancing the zebras that meander the huge scene. This people group, known as the Zebra Heroes, is in excess of a gathering of people — it is an embroidery of lives woven together by customs, shared encounters, and a profound association with the land. In this investigation, we dive into the appearances behind the Zebra Heroes, uncovering the rich embroidered artwork of their lives, customs, and the persevering through soul that characterizes their one of a kind personality.

Starting points and Legacy:

The underlying foundations of the Zebra Fighters stretch back through ages, a demonstration of the perseverance of social practices despite an influencing world. Passed down from predecessors who explored similar savannah, the legacy of the Zebra Heroes is a living inheritance, conveying with it the insight of the people who preceded.

Elderly folks, worshipped for their experience and information, are the watchmen of this social legacy. Through narrating, functions, and the passing down of customs, they guarantee that the embodiment of the Zebra Fighter character stays in one piece. Each face locally holds a section of this living history, interfacing the past, present, and future in a consistent continuum.

Local area Bonds:

At the core of the Zebra Champions is a significant feeling of local area, where each face assumes a urgent part in the aggregate embroidery. In the Get-together of the Group, a collective occasion where stories are shared, giggling reverberations, and bonds are reinforced, faces light up with the glow of shared encounters. The strength of the Zebra Fighters lies in their solidarity, a power that rises above individual countenances to frame an aggregate soul.

This feeling of local area stretches out past familial ties, enveloping an organization of connections that jumble the savannah. Faces, endured by the sun and set apart by the progression of time, mirror the interconnectedness that characterizes the Zebra Champion lifestyle. Whether in the midst of festivity or confronting difficulties, the local area remains as a tough trap of help.

Countenances of Flexibility:

The savannah, with its capricious weather conditions, moving scenes, and the consistently present dance of hunter and prey, requests strength. The countenances behind the Zebra Champions give testimony regarding the difficulties presented commonly, outside pressures, and the unique balance of life on the savannah.

Endured at this point faithful, these countenances typify the soul of transformation and versatility. From changing relocation courses notwithstanding changing environment examples to fighting off outer dangers, the Zebra Heroes stand as a demonstration of the unyielding human soul. In their eyes, one sees the impression of ages who have endured storms, confronted difficulty, and arose more grounded, their versatility carved into the lines on their appearances.

The Dance of Stripes:

Social practices are carved into the actual texture of the Zebra Fighters' presence, and no place is this more apparent than in the Dance of Stripes. A formal exhibition that reflects the developments of zebras across the savannah, this dance isn't only a scene — it is a representative articulation of the solidarity, variety, and congruity that characterize the Zebra Champion people group.

Faces decorated with stately paint, bodies moving together as one, the Dance of Stripes is a living material that recounts a story. Every member adds to this living workmanship, their appearances enlivened with the soul of festivity and social pride. In the Dance of Stripes, custom and development cross, making a unique articulation of personality that reverberates across the savannah.

Functions and Soul changing experiences:

Life among the Zebra Champions is interspersed by services that mark huge achievements and soul changing experiences. From the commencement of youthful champions to functions respecting the older, each face locally conveys the engravings of these consecrated minutes.

The essences of youthful fighters, decorated with images of their newly discovered liabilities, mirror the expectation and energy of leaving on an excursion of self-revelation. Elderly folks, faces scratched with a truly mind-blowing insight, are respected in services that recognize their job as mainstays of the local area. These soul changing experiences shape individual ways of life as well as add to the aggregate account of the Zebra Champions.

Ecological Stewardship:

The countenances behind the Zebra Heroes are the caretakers of social practices as well as the stewards of the land they call home. With a profound comprehension of the interconnectedness among mankind and nature, the Zebra Heroes effectively take part in ecological protection rehearses.

Faces spread with dirt, hands keeping an eye on the dirt, the Zebra Fighters utilize supportable rural practices that guarantee the soundness of the land. They perceive that their prosperity is unpredictably connected to the prosperity of the savannah, and their countenances mirror a guarantee to safeguarding the fragile equilibrium of the biological system.

Difficulties of the Cutting edge World:

As their general surroundings develops, the essences of the Zebra Champions face the difficulties of innovation. Globalization, environmental change, and outer tensions present vulnerabilities that require key reasoning and versatility. The Zebra Champions should explore the sensitive harmony between safeguarding their social legacy and embracing components of the advanced world.

The essences of youthful fighters, naturally introduced to a world molded by innovation and interconnected worldwide frameworks, mirror the duality of this presence. They wrestle with the strain among custom and innovation, looking for ways of regarding their social heritage while exploring the potential open doors and intricacies of the contemporary world.

Schooling and Passing the Light:

Schooling is an encouraging sign for the Zebra Champions, a pathway for the transmission of information and the strengthening of people in the future. Countenances of youthful students, anxious to ingest the insight of their older folks, mirror the coherence of the Zebra Champion heritage. Training turns into a scaffold among custom and progress, guaranteeing that the countenances behind the Zebra Heroes are prepared to address the difficulties representing things to come.

The death of the light, starting with one age then onto the next, is a powerful second that works out in the essences of guides and mentees. Seniors, faces aglow with the fulfillment of conferring information, guide the following influx of pioneers who will convey the social light forward. This intergenerational trade is a foundation of the Zebra Champion people group, guaranteeing the conservation of customs while encouraging development.

Financial Supportability and Worldwide Coordinated effort:

Notwithstanding financial vulnerabilities and worldwide changes, the countenances behind the Zebra Heroes explore pathways to monetary manageability.

Local area based protection and mindful the travel industry drives become wellsprings of income as well as stages for imparting their social legacy to the world.

The essences of Zebra Champions drawing in with guests mirror a guarantee to worldwide coordinated effort and multifaceted comprehension. By making their ways for dependable the travel industry, they make spans that interface their local area with the more extensive worldwide woven artwork. Monetary maintainability becomes entwined with social safeguarding, building up the possibility that the countenances behind the Zebra Heroes are representatives of a special lifestyle.

Planning ahead:

As the countenances behind the Zebra Heroes look into the distance, they see a future that holds the two difficulties and potential open doors. The embroidery they weave is dynamic, intelligent of a local area that embraces change while defending its social roots. The Zebra Fighters stand at the convergence of custom and innovation, confronting the intricacies of the 21st 100 years with a soul manufactured by hundreds of years of flexibility.

According to the Zebra Champions, there is an impression of trust — an expectation that their social heritage will persevere, that the savannah they call home will stay a flourishing biological system, and that people in the future will acquire a reality where the dance of stripes proceeds. The countenances behind the Zebra Champions typify an immortal soul, one that reverberations across the tremendous spread of the African savannah, making a permanent imprint on the scene and in the hearts of the people who experience their story.

3.1 Profiles of Key Founders and Leaders

In the core of the African savannah, the Zebra Champions find their solidarity and strength directed by the visionaries who established and lead their extraordinary local area. These critical originators and pioneers, with a profound association with custom and a forward-looking point of view, assume significant parts in controlling the Zebra Heroes through the intricacies of the cutting edge world. In this investigation, we dive into the profiles of these visionary people, understanding the stories that have formed their authority and the effect they've had on the social embroidered artwork of the Zebra Heroes.

1. **Authority Nia Mbali:**

   At the core of the Zebra Fighters stands Matron Nia Mbali, a lady of shrewdness and strength who encapsulates the hereditary soul of the local area. Nia Mbali, which means "Mother of Blossoms" in the nearby language, is respected for her profound comprehension of the land, customs, and the interconnectedness of every living thing.

   Naturally introduced to a genealogy of profound pioneers, Nia Mbali expected her job as the matron after a progression of dreams and dreams that she accepts were messages from the spirits of the savannah. Her authority is established in a significant regard for nature, and she has been instrumental in encouraging a feeling of ecological stewardship among the Zebra Champions.

   Nia Mbali's vision reaches out past the limits of the local area. She has effectively drawn in with global protection associations, supporting for feasible practices and the conservation of the savannah environment. Nia Mbali's initiative is described by an agreeable mix of custom and development, guaranteeing that the Zebra Heroes explore the difficulties of the cutting edge world while remaining consistent with their social legacy.

2. **Boss Sipho Malenga:**

   Boss Sipho Malenga is the overseer of the Zebra Champions' social legacy, a charming pioneer known for his capacity to join the local area through narrating and function. Brought into the world under the shade of an old acacia tree, Boss

Malenga grew up submerged in the rich oral practices of the Zebra Fighters. His initiative is characterized by a guarantee to saving and passing on the social tradition of the local area. Boss Malenga has been instrumental in restoring antiquated services, including the Dance of Stripes and transitional experiences that mark huge achievements in the existences of local area individuals. Under his direction, the Zebra Fighters have laid out a social place to record and exhibit their practices, guaranteeing that people in the future have a substantial association with their foundations.

Boss Malenga is likewise an extension between the Zebra Heroes and the rest of the world. He has taken part in social trade programs, welcoming researchers, craftsmen, and specialists to encounter the exceptional lifestyle in the savannah. Through these trades, Boss Malenga plans to cultivate a more profound comprehension of the Zebra Champions' way of life and to counter generalizations frequently connected with native networks.

3. **Senior Kofi Jelani:**

Senior Kofi Jelani, with a face endured by many years of living together as one with the savannah, is the storehouse of natural information inside the Zebra Heroes. Brought into the world during a time of bountiful downpours, Kofi Jelani fostered an early interest with the verdure that encompassed his local area.

As a senior, Kofi Jelani is the gatekeeper of economical asset the board rehearses. He plays had a significant impact in creating procedures for capable land use, water preservation, and conventional farming that line up with the environmental equilibrium of the savannah.

Kofi Jelani's face mirrors the lived encounters of adjusting to the changing environment designs and the difficulties presented by outer tensions on the land.

Notwithstanding his environmental skill, Kofi Jelani is a coach to the more youthful age, passing on the multifaceted information on plant medication and the fragile transaction among people and the different species that occupy the savannah. His vision is grounded in the conviction that an agreeable conjunction with nature is fundamental for the prosperity of the Zebra Champions and the manageability of their lifestyle.

4. **Youth Pioneer Amina Nyota:**

Amina Nyota, a lively and dynamic youth pioneer, addresses the forward-looking soul of the Zebra Heroes. Brought into the world under the look of a full moon, Amina grew up with an oddity about the world past the savannah. Her initiative style is portrayed by a combination of customary qualities and a strong fascination with utilizing innovation and training to address the difficulties looked by the local area.

Amina has been a main impetus behind local area based training drives, pushing for the reconciliation of conventional information with current subjects. She imagines a future where the young people of the Zebra Fighters are not just knowledgeable in that frame of mind of their progenitors yet in addition furnished with the abilities expected to draw in with the more extensive world-wide local area.

As a team with worldwide accomplices, Amina has led projects zeroed in on manageable turn of events and youth strengthening. She trusts that by embracing development while remaining established in custom, the Zebra Champions can make a model for strong, socially rich networks in the 21st 100 years.

5. **Profound Aide Kwame Ngoma:**

Profound Aide Kwame Ngoma, with a face enhanced with emblematic markings, is the otherworldly anchor of the Zebra Champions. Brought into the world during a lunar obscuration, Kwame Ngoma showed an association with the profound domain since the beginning. His job as an aide includes deciphering dreams, speaking with the spirits of the savannah, and directing functions that honor the tribal powers.

Kwame Ngoma's initiative is profoundly interwoven with the otherworldly prosperity of the local area. He assumes a focal part in ceremonies that summon the gifts of the spirits for the success and security of the Zebra Champions. His face, painted with sacrosanct images, mirrors a significant otherworldly excursion that lines up with the patterns of nature.

Past the local area, Kwame Ngoma has participated in interfaith exchanges, cultivating a comprehension of the profound acts of the Zebra Champions. He accepts that otherworldliness is a bringing together power that rises above social limits and can possibly advance congruity in a world wrestling with divisions.

6. **Local area Negotiator Zara Tembo:**

Zara Tembo, known as the local area negotiator, is a scaffold between the Zebra Fighters and the more extensive worldwide local area. Brought into the world during a time of relocation, Zara grew up with a characteristic tendency for building associations and figuring out the points of view of others.

Her position of authority includes addressing the Zebra Champions in global discussions, drawing in with protection associations, and supporting for the privileges and prosperity of native networks. Zara's face mirrors a mix of social pride and a cosmopolitan viewpoint, representing the interconnectedness of the Zebra Champions with the worldwide embroidery.

Zara has been instrumental in fashioning associations that benefit the local area monetarily while guaranteeing the safeguarding of social qualities. She accepts that by effectively taking part in worldwide discussions, the Zebra Fighters can add to the discourse on supportable turn of events, ecological preservation, and the significance of saving native societies.

Inheritance and Cooperative Vision:

These vital pioneers and heads of the Zebra Heroes, each with an interesting profile and commitment, team up to wind around an embroidery that praises custom, embraces development, and imagines a practical future. Their initiative isn't solitary yet rises up out of an aggregate obligation to the prosperity of the local area and the protection of a social inheritance that traverses ages.

Together, they have fabricated an inheritance that reaches out past the savannah — a heritage that welcomes coordinated effort, understanding, and common regard. Their countenances, carved with the tales of the Zebra Champions, mirror a common vision for an existence where various societies coincide agreeably, where the insight of the past educates the decisions regarding the present, and where administration is grounded in a profound love for the interconnected trap of life. As the Zebra Champions proceed with their excursion, directed by these visionary chiefs, they convey with them the expectation that their exceptional lifestyle will persevere, flourish, and motivate others to proceed with caution on the Earth.

3.2Stories of Dedicated Conservationists

In the continuous fight to safeguard the fragile equilibrium of our planet's environments, committed preservationists arise as overlooked yet truly great individuals, vigorously attempting to safeguard biodiversity, reestablish living spaces, and guarantee a feasible future for a long time into the future. These people, driven by an enthusiasm for nature and a promise to ecological stewardship, weave accounts of flexibility, development, and unfaltering assurance. In this investigation, we dig into the motivating stories of protectionists who have become watchmen of biodiversity and stewards of the Earth.

1. **Dr. Jane Goodall: The Exploring Primatologist:**
   No conversation of committed protectionists would be finished without referencing Dr. Jane Goodall, an exploring primatologist whose work with chimpanzees reformed how we might interpret creature conduct and protection. In 1960, at 26 years old, Goodall wandered into the Gombe Stream Public Park in Tanzania to concentrate on wild chimpanzees.

   Throughout the long term, Goodall's exploration reshaped how we might interpret primates as well as featured the critical requirement for protection endeavors. Seeing the dangers looked by chimpanzees because of deforestation, natural surroundings misfortune, and poaching, Goodall turned into a wild promoter for their security. The Jane Goodall Establishment, established in 1977, centers around local area focused protection, supporting natural surroundings safeguarding, and enabling neighborhood networks to be stewards of their current circumstance.

   Jane Goodall's story is one of unflinching commitment, as she keeps on venturing to the far corners of the planet, motivating the up and coming age of protectionists. Her message rises above the domain of science, underlining the interconnectedness of every single living being and the significant effect every individual can have in the world.

2. **Wangari Maathai: The Green Belt Development's Visionary:**

Wangari Maathai, a visionary Kenyan earthy person, established the Green Belt Development in 1977, a grassroots association that advances natural preservation, ladies' freedoms, and local area improvement. Maathai's story is one of fortitude and strength notwithstanding natural corruption and social unfairness.

Perceiving the interconnectedness of natural issues and human prosperity, Maathai drove the Green Belt Development in establishing a great many trees across Kenya. This reforestation drive countered deforestation as well as enabled ladies by furnishing them with pay producing potential open doors.

Wangari Maathai's obligation to natural protection and civil rights acquired her the Nobel Harmony Prize in 2004, making her the main African lady to get this honor. Her inheritance lives on through the Green Belt Development, which keeps on establishing trees, engage networks, and supporter for practical turn of events.

3. **Dr. Sylvia Earle: The Oceanographer and Marine Traditionalist:**
   Dr. Sylvia Earle, a spearheading oceanographer and sea life scholar, has committed her life to investigating the profundities of the sea and pushing for its insurance. Known as "Her Profundity," Earle's commitments to marine protection are both logical and rousing.

   Earle's broad examination, remembering driving the main group of ladies aquanauts for 1970, has developed how we might interpret marine environments. In any case, her responsibility stretches out past scholarly community.

   As a backer for sea preservation, Earle established Mission Blue, an association devoted to making marine safeguarded regions, or "Trust Spots," all over the planet.

   Sylvia Earle's story is one of investigation and support, underlining the basic job seas play in supporting life on The planet. Through her determined endeavors, she has propelled a worldwide development to safeguard the "blue heart" of our planet and protect the marvels concealed underneath the waves.

4. **Dr. Russell Mittermeier: The Primatologist and Biodiversity Champion:**
   Dr. Russell Mittermeier, a primatologist and eminent biodiversity master, has devoted his vocation to the review and protection of imperiled species. Mittermeier's attention on primates has taken him to the remote corners of the world, where he has worked resolutely to archive and safeguard these weak animals.

   As the leader of Protection Worldwide, Mittermeier has been instrumental in propelling preservation techniques that focus on the conservation of biodiversity areas of interest. His methodology accentuates the significance of safeguarding whole environments to protect the bunch species that rely upon them.

   Russell Mittermeier's story is one of logical thoroughness and a profound obligation to biodiversity preservation. Through his examination, support, and initiative, he has turned into a worldwide voice for the security of jeopardized species and the conservation of the planet's most compromised natural surroundings.

5. **Dr. Vandana Shiva: The Natural Extremist and Seed Power Backer:**

Dr. Vandana Shiva, a natural lobbyist and physicist, has turned into a main voice in the worldwide development for manageable horticulture and seed sway. Her process is set apart by a savage obligation to environmental trustworthiness, civil rights, and the strengthening of ranchers.

Through the association Navdanya, established in 1987, Shiva has supported the security of biodiversity, upholding for customary cultivating rehearses and the protection of local seeds. Her work underlines the interconnectedness of farming, biodiversity, and the prosperity of networks.

Vandana Shiva's story is one of activism and support, testing the predominance of modern horticulture and advancing a regenerative and comprehensive way to deal with cultivating. As a protector of seed sway, she highlights the significance of safeguarding customary information and engaging ranchers to be stewards of the land.

6. **Dr. Carl Safina: The Biologist and Backer for Sea Preservation:**

Dr. Carl Safina, a biologist, creator, and backer for sea preservation, has devoted his vocation to figuring out marine environments and imparting the criticalness of safeguarding our seas.

Safina's work overcomes any barrier between logical examination and public mindfulness, making complex natural issues open to a more extensive crowd.

As the organizer behind the Safina Center, Carl Safina centers around propelling protection drives through science, craftsmanship, and writing. His narrating approach features the interconnectedness of human and sea life, cultivating sympathy and a feeling of obligation for the strength of our oceans.

Safina's story is one of correspondence and support, exhibiting the force of account to motivate change. By drawing in the general population and policymakers the same, he tries to make an existence where the seas, overflowing with life, are safeguarded and loved to support momentum and people in the future

3.3 The Team Behind the Success: Scientists, Activists, and Volunteers

In the realm of natural preservation, achievement is much of the time the consequence of an aggregate exertion — an orchestra of committed people working as one to safeguard our planet's biodiversity and address squeezing biological difficulties. This cooperative power incorporates researchers leading earth shattering exploration, activists supporting for change, and volunteers contributing their significant investment on the bleeding edges. In this investigation, we dig into the jobs of researchers, activists, and volunteers — the powerful group behind the progress of natural protection drives.

1. **Researchers: The Designers of Information and Revelation:**

At the very front of ecological preservation are researchers, the engineers of information and revelation who disentangle the secrets of the normal world. Their work includes a wide range, from concentrating on environments and inventoriing biodiversity to exploring the effect of environmental change on weak species. Through thorough logical request, they give the establishment whereupon powerful protection systems are fabricated.

Researchers add to preservation in different ways:

Biodiversity Exploration: Researchers lead field studies, biodiversity appraisals, and hereditary investigations to grasp the complexities of environments. Their work frequently includes distinguishing key species, surveying populace elements, and planning environments.

Environmental Change Exploration: Natural researchers examine the effect of environmental change on biological systems and species. This remembers reading up shifts for movement designs, modifications in vegetation, and the reaction of natural life to changing ecological circumstances.

Inventive Arrangements: Researchers foster creative answers for protection challenges. This might include making feasible innovations, executing natural life global positioning frameworks, or creating protection hereditary qualities strategies to safeguard hereditary variety.

Strategy and Backing: Numerous researchers effectively participate in arrangement and support endeavors, utilizing their examination discoveries to illuminate leaders and backer for proof based natural approaches.

Crafted by researchers is urgent for laying out a hearty comprehension of the difficulties confronting our planet and creating informed, proof based techniques for preservation. By extending our insight base, researchers assume a critical part in forming the direction of natural drives.

2. **Activists: The Voices for Change and Support:**

Activists are the enthusiastic voices for change, energetically upholding for the assurance of the climate and the privileges of the planet's occupants. Whether in the city, in meeting rooms, or on computerized stages, activists bring issues to light, challenge hurtful practices, and champion the reason for ecological equity. Their promotion reaches out indeed; a source of inspiration tries to prepare people, networks, and organizations.

Key commitments of natural activists include:

Bringing issues to light: Activists focus on natural issues, utilizing different stages to educate general society about the earnestness regarding preservation. Through missions, narratives, and grassroots developments, they focus on dangers like deforestation, contamination, and loss of biodiversity.

Local area Commitment: Activists work intimately with networks impacted by ecological issues, enabling them to be advocates for their own prosperity. This incorporates working together on supportable advancement projects, advancing eco-accommodating practices, and intensifying the voices of minimized networks.

Corporate Responsibility: Natural activists consider companies responsible for their ecological effect. Through designated missions, blacklists, and investor activism, they push for feasible strategic policies and challenge enterprises adding to ecological corruption.

Strategy Support: Activists draw in with policymakers to impact regulation and guidelines that influence the climate. They advocate for more grounded natural assurances, the authorization of existing regulations, and the reception of feasible practices at neighborhood, public, and worldwide levels.

Activists assume a urgent part in catalyzing cultural change and making a groundswell of help for ecological protection. Their energy and responsibility act as a main impetus, convincing people and organizations to reconsider their effect in the world and embrace more reasonable practices.

3. **Volunteers: The Hands and Hearts on the Bleeding edges:**

Volunteers are the hands and hearts on the bleeding edges of preservation endeavors, devoting their time, energy, and skill to help a great many drives. From tree planting and natural surroundings rebuilding to untamed life checking and local area outreach, volunteers structure the foundation of numerous preservation projects. Their commitments, frequently determined by a profound feeling of obligation and love for the climate, are important in carrying out on-the-ground arrangements.

Key jobs and commitments of natural workers include:

Territory Rebuilding: Volunteers effectively partake in living space reclamation projects, establishing trees, eliminating obtrusive species, and restoring biological systems. Their endeavors add to the recovery of corrupted regions and the production of better territories for untamed life.

Natural life Checking: Numerous protection programs depend on volunteers to screen natural life populaces, track relocation examples, and gather information on species overflow. This data is urgent for figuring out the wellbeing of environments and distinguishing regions needing insurance.

Local area Effort: Volunteers draw in with neighborhood networks to advance natural mindfulness, training, and feasible practices. They work with studios, sort out tidy up occasions, and encourage a feeling of natural stewardship inside networks.

Crisis Reaction: despite cataclysmic events or natural crises, chips in frequently assume a basic part accordingly and recuperation endeavors. Their fast assembly and active help offer prompt help to impacted biological systems and untamed life.

Volunteers exemplify the soul of grassroots activity, making an interpretation of enthusiasm into unmistakable outcomes on the ground. Their different abilities and foundations add to the multi-layered nature of preservation drives, and their aggregate effect is a demonstration of the force of local area driven endeavors.

Cooperation and Collaboration:

The progress of natural protection depends on the collaboration between researchers, activists, and volunteers. At the point when these powers join together, a strong alliance arises — one that consolidates logical skill, support, and grassroots activity to impact significant change. The cooperative idea of this group guarantees that preservation endeavors are educated by information and exploration as well as implanted in the texture of networks and driven by a common obligation to the planet.

As we explore the difficulties of a quickly impacting world, the group behind the outcome of ecological protection proceeds to develop and grow. The consideration of different voices, abilities, and viewpoints reinforces the versatility of these aggregate endeavors, offering expect a future where mankind lives as one with the Earth. In this aggregate undertaking, researchers, activists, and volunteers stand joined as watchmen of biodiversity, stewards of the Earth, and heroes of a manageable future.

Chapter 4

Challenges and Triumphs

Ecological protection is a respectable undertaking, driven by the basic to defend the fragile equilibrium of our planet's environments. As mankind wrestles with the results of environmental change, territory misfortune, contamination, and the exhaustion of regular assets, the difficulties confronting protectionists have never been more mind boggling. However, inside this embroidery of impediments lie accounts of win — occurrences where committed people, networks, and associations have resisted the chances to have a beneficial outcome on the climate. In this investigation, we dig into the difficulties that natural progressives defy and the victories that enlighten the way towards a practical future.

Challenges:

Environmental Change and A worldwide temperature alteration:

Environmental change, driven by the ascent in ozone depleting substance emanations, presents one of the main difficulties to ecological preservation. The World's environment is going through significant movements, prompting climbing temperatures, adjusted precipitation examples, and more continuous outrageous climate occasions. These progressions influence environments, upset movement designs, and compromise the endurance of innumerable species.

Alleviating environmental change requires worldwide participation to lessen outflows, progress to sustainable power sources, and adjust to the evolving conditions. Preservationists face the test of pushing for and executing approaches that address the main drivers of environmental change while likewise creating systems to safeguard weak environments and species.

Natural surroundings Misfortune and Fracture:

Human exercises, like deforestation, urbanization, and horticulture, keep on infringing upon normal natural surroundings, prompting living space misfortune and fracture. This represents an immediate danger to biodiversity, as numerous species rely upon explicit natural surroundings for endurance. Fracture disturbs movement courses, confines populaces, and decreases the accessibility of assets.

Protection endeavors should address the double test of safeguarding existing environments and reestablishing debased ones. This includes working with neighborhood networks, executing manageable land-use rehearses, and pushing for the assurance of basic biological systems. Moreover, the making of untamed life passages and safeguarded regions is fundamental to reconnect divided territories.

Loss of Biodiversity:

The speeding up loss of biodiversity is a worldwide emergency with expansive ramifications for biological systems and human prosperity. Annihilation rates are alarmingly high, determined by elements like environment obliteration, contamination, overexploitation, and the presentation of obtrusive species. The deficiency of biodiversity subverts the strength of environments, upsets established pecking orders, and decreases the potential for logical and clinical revelations got from assorted species.

Progressives wrestle with the test of forestalling further species misfortune and reestablishing populaces of jeopardized plants and creatures. This includes living space preservation, hostage rearing projects, and endeavors to battle unlawful untamed life exchange. Furthermore, there is a requirement for public mindfulness missions to underline the interconnectedness of all species and the significance of saving biodiversity.

Contamination and Natural Pollution:

Contamination, whether from modern releases, farming spillover, plastic waste, or synthetic pollutants, represents an unavoidable danger to biological systems and human wellbeing. It debases air and water quality, hurts oceanic life, and adds to the downfall of biodiversity. Plastic contamination, specifically, has turned into a worldwide emergency, with immense measures of plastic waste collecting in seas and earthbound conditions.

Tending to contamination requires a diverse methodology, including stricter guidelines, squander the board foundation, and government funded instruction on reasonable utilization. Protectionists pursue bringing issues to light about the effect of contamination on biological systems, upholding for strategy changes, and supporting drives that advance a roundabout economy and decrease dependence on single-use plastics.

Overexploitation of Regular Assets:

The impractical abuse of normal assets, whether through overfishing, unlawful logging, or the extraction of minerals, exhausts environments and upsets natural equilibrium. Overfishing, for instance, compromises marine biodiversity as well as endangers the vocations of networks subject to fisheries.

Moderates face the test of advancing feasible asset the board rehearses that offset human necessities with the safeguarding of environments. This incorporates pushing for capable fishing works on, supporting local area based preservation drives, and advancing maintainable ranger service and agribusiness. Joint effort with neighborhood networks is fundamental to guarantee that preservation techniques line up with the requirements and desires of the individuals who rely upon regular assets.

Wins:

Reforestation and Territory Reclamation:

Because of the test of broad deforestation, various reforestation and natural surroundings rebuilding drives have made amazing progress. Associations and networks all over the planet have met up to establish a great many trees, reestablish debased scenes, and make natural surroundings halls. These endeavors add to carbon sequestration as well as rejuvenate biological systems and give basic environments to different species.

An outstanding victory is the Incomparable Green Wall project in Africa, where nations are cooperating to battle desertification by establishing a mosaic of trees and vegetation. This drive grandstands the potential for enormous scope, cooperative reforestation ventures to address environment misfortune and relieve the effects of environmental change.

Safeguarded Regions and Preservation Stores:

The foundation of safeguarded regions and protection holds has demonstrated viable in saving basic territories and defending biodiversity. Public parks, marine stores, and untamed life safe-havens act as shelters for imperiled species and permit biological systems to recuperate from human-prompted unsettling influences.

Examples of overcoming adversity remember the restoration of untamed life populaces for Yellowstone Public Park after the renewed introduction of wolves, and the recuperation of marine life in safeguarded regions, for example, the Incomparable Boundary Reef Marine Park. These victories highlight the significance of saving regions where nature can flourish without the immediate tensions of human abuse.

Local area Based Preservation:

Engaging neighborhood networks to play a functioning job in protection has arisen as a fruitful procedure. Local area based preservation drives connect with occupants in reasonable asset the board, natural surroundings reclamation, and untamed life security. This approach perceives the significance of integrating native information and including networks as stewards of their nearby surroundings.

Projects like the Namibian People group Based Regular Asset The board Program feature how engaging neighborhood networks can prompt fruitful protection results. By adjusting preservation objectives to the interests of networks, these drives encourage a feeling of pride and obligation regarding the prosperity of the two individuals and nature.

Advancements in Innovation:

Headways in innovation have opened new wildernesses in ecological protection. From satellite symbolism for checking deforestation to acoustic observing for following untamed life, mechanical developments give significant instruments to progressives. Drones, camera traps, and information examination empower more proficient and extensive checking of biological systems and species.

Wins in preservation innovation incorporate the utilization of computerized reasoning to break down huge datasets, considering quicker and more exact recognizable proof of imperiled species. These mechanical headways upgrade the accuracy and viability of protection endeavors, furnishing traditionalists with the apparatuses they need to address complex difficulties.

Worldwide Protection Joint efforts:

Worldwide joint efforts and arrangements play had a vital impact in tending to worldwide ecological difficulties. Deals, for example, the Show on Natural Variety and the Paris Settlement on environmental change exhibit the potential for aggregate activity on a worldwide scale. These arrangements unite countries to share information, set targets, and resolve to composed endeavors for natural manageability.

Examples of overcoming adversity incorporate the Montreal Convention, a global settlement pointed toward eliminating ozone-exhausting substances. The aggregate endeavors of countries prompted a huge decrease in the utilization of hurtful synthetic substances, adding to the recuperation of the ozone layer. These cooperative victories underscore the requirement for a unified worldwide reaction to shared ecological difficulties.

4.1 Obstacles Faced by Zebra Warriors

In the core of the African savannah, the Zebra Champions stand as watchmen of their social legacy and stewards of the regular world. However, this respectable pursuit isn't without its difficulties. The Zebra Heroes, a local area profoundly associated with the land and its customs, face a heap of impediments as they endeavor to adjust the protection of their lifestyle with the developing elements of the contemporary world. In this investigation, we dive into the hindrances looked by the Zebra Heroes, revealing insight into the intricacies of social protection and ecological preservation in the 21st hundred years.

Environment Fracture and Misfortune:

One of the essential difficulties looked by the Zebra Heroes is territory fracture and misfortune. As human populaces extend and land-use designs change, the customary domains of the Zebra Fighters are progressively infringed upon. The once huge and interconnected scenes that supported their lifestyle are presently divided by streets, settlements, and agrarian exercises. This discontinuity upsets the normal movement examples of natural life, influencing the sensitive equilibrium of the savannah biological system.

The Zebra Heroes, who have depended on the land for a really long time, end up exploring a scene that is quickly changing. The deficiency of coterminous territories undermines the biodiversity of the savannah as well as postures difficulties to conventional practices like the Dance of Stripes — a stately custom complicatedly connected to the regular rhythms of the land.

Environmental Change and Natural Interruptions:

The ghost of environmental change poses a potential threat over the African savannah, carrying with it erratic weather conditions, delayed dry seasons, and outrageous temperatures. The Zebra Heroes, personally sensitive to the patterns of nature, face the test of adjusting to these quick biological disturbances. Changes in precipitation designs influence the accessibility of water sources, essential for both untamed life and the Zebra Heroes themselves.

The itinerant way of life of the Zebra Fighters, once fit with the anticipated patterns of the savannah, is currently defied with the vulnerability achieved by environmental change. Customary information went down through ages should now be rethought even with moving biological elements, requesting a sensitive harmony between safeguarding social practices and adjusting to ecological real factors.

Tension from Outer Impacts:

The Zebra Champions wind up under expanding tension from outside impacts, including the infringement of innovation and the impact of globalized societies. As their general surroundings changes, the Zebra Champions wrestle with the deluge of outside thoughts, innovations, and worth frameworks. The charm of metropolitan ways of life, formal instruction, and financial open doors outside the savannah represents a test to the conventional itinerant lifestyle.

The more youthful age of Zebra Heroes, specifically, faces the back-and-forth between the social legacy of their predecessors and the charm of an additional cutting edge and associated world. Adjusting the protection of their one of a kind character with the tensions of outer impacts turns into a fragile dance — one that requires smart route to guarantee the progression of Zebra Hero customs.

Natural life Preservation Difficulties:

As stewards of the savannah, the Zebra Champions are unpredictably connected to the prosperity of the natural life that occupies their genealogical grounds. Be that as it may, the difficulties looked by natural life — going from poaching and environment corruption to human-natural life clashes — represent extra snags for the Zebra Heroes. The decrease in natural life populaces, including notable species like zebras, challenges the social importance and biological equilibrium that the Zebra Heroes have long kept up with.

Endeavors to address untamed life protection challenges frequently include exploring complex associations with outside elements, like government offices, non-administrative associations (NGOs), and worldwide preservation drives. The Zebra Champions end up in a position where they should advocate for the security of their sacrosanct scenes and the animals that possess them while arranging the more extensive scene of protection endeavors.

Monetary Tensions and Economical Livelihoods:

The customary jobs of the Zebra Heroes, established in roaming pastoralism and a manageable relationship with the land, are progressively stressed by monetary tensions. Worldwide monetary elements, market requests, and the requirement for cash pay in an adapted world make difficulties for a local area that has generally flourished with independence.

As the Zebra Champions investigate ways of adjusting to changing monetary scenes, they should proceed cautiously to guarantee that financial open doors line up with their upsides of natural stewardship and social safeguarding. Manageable job choices that permit the Zebra Heroes to keep up with their association with the land while meeting contemporary financial necessities become pivotal in exploring this deterrent.

Wins and Arrangements:

Social Versatility and Transformation:

While the Zebra Heroes face imposing deterrents, their story isn't one of rout yet rather an account of social versatility and transformation. The people group has shown a momentous capacity to adjust to changing conditions while protecting the center fundamentals of their social character. Through a unique interaction of custom and development, the Zebra Champions have tracked down ways of incorporating parts of innovation without compromising the embodiment of their lifestyle.

Drives, for example, local area drove social celebrations, narrating occasions, and the renewal of customary services grandstand the Zebra Champions' obligation to social versatility. By effectively captivating with more youthful ages and outer impacts, the local area looks to guarantee the congruity of their social legacy despite developing difficulties.

Local area Based Protection Practices:

Perceiving the interconnectedness of their prosperity with the strength of the savannah, the Zebra Champions have embraced local area based preservation rehearses. These drives include dynamic support in natural life checking, territory reclamation projects, and feasible land-use rehearses. By taking responsibility for endeavors, the Zebra Champions adjust their social qualities to environmental stewardship.

Coordinated efforts with protection associations and administrative offices have permitted the Zebra Champions to incorporate conventional information with present day preservation systems. The foundation of local area oversaw protection regions and the execution of maintainable asset the executives plans embody the local area's obligation to guaranteeing the biological honesty of their genealogical grounds.

Training and Strengthening:

In tending to the difficulties presented by outside impacts, the Zebra Heroes have perceived the significance of schooling and strengthening. Drives to give formal instruction, while as yet regarding the local area's itinerant way of life, engage the more youthful age with the abilities and information expected to explore both customary and contemporary universes.

Schooling turns into an instrument for strengthening, empowering the Zebra Champions to draw in with outside impacts according to their very own preferences effectively. By encouraging a feeling of satisfaction in their social legacy and outfitting the more youthful age with the devices to explore outside pressures, the Zebra Fighters guarantee that their heritage perseveres despite developing scenes.

Social Discretion and Promotion:

In the domain of untamed life preservation, the Zebra Heroes have arisen as backers for the security of their sacrosanct scenes and the animals that possess them. Participating in social strategy, the local area effectively conveys the significance of their social practices in keeping up with the biological equilibrium of the savannah. This promotion brings issues to light as well as lays out the Zebra Champions as key partners in more extensive protection conversations.

Through essential coordinated efforts with legislative bodies, NGOs, and worldwide accomplices, the Zebra Champions influence their social information to illuminate and shape protection strategies. This proactive commitment positions the local area as imperative supporters of the economical administration of the savannah, building up the possibility that social protection and natural preservation are indivisible.

4.2 Success Stories Despite Challenges

In the domain of natural protection and social safeguarding, examples of overcoming adversity frequently arise as encouraging signs, showing that even notwithstanding imposing difficulties, positive change is conceivable. Across the globe, networks, associations, and people have explored deterrents going from environmental change and living space misfortune to social disintegration and financial tensions.

In this investigation, we dig into examples of overcoming adversity that stand apart in the midst of affliction, displaying the versatility and creativity of the people who have conquered difficulties to accomplish significant results in both natural protection and social conservation.

Gorongosa Public Park, Mozambique:

Challenges Confronted:

Gorongosa Public Park in Mozambique confronted critical difficulties, including many years of common turmoil, poaching, and environment obliteration. The recreation area's untamed life, when plentiful, experienced serious downfalls, and the environmental equilibrium was disturbed.

Example of overcoming adversity:

In spite of these difficulties, the reclamation of Gorongosa Public Park remains as a striking example of overcoming adversity. The Carr Establishment, as a team with the Mozambican government, set out on an aggressive venture to revive the recreation area. Mediations included enemy of poaching endeavors, environment reclamation, and local area commitment programs.

One of the key achievement factors was the joining of nearby networks into the preservation endeavors. Local area drove drives, for example, supportable horticulture projects and eco-the travel industry undertakings, gave financial open doors as well as encouraged a feeling of pride and stewardship among the neighborhood populace.

The reclamation endeavors have yielded amazing outcomes, with natural life populaces bouncing back, including notable species like elephants and lions. The progress of Gorongosa Public Park outlines the groundbreaking force of cooperative, local area based preservation approaches in reviving environments and shielding biodiversity.

Sámi Reindeer Crowding, Scandinavia:

Challenges Confronted:

The Sámi public, native to the Icy areas of Scandinavia, confronted difficulties to their customary reindeer grouping rehearses. Environmental change, foundation advancement, and modern exercises upset the transient courses of reindeer, compromising the Sámi lifestyle.

Example of overcoming adversity:

Even with these difficulties, the Sámi public have utilized creative techniques to adjust and protect their social practices. One eminent achievement is the utilization of present day innovation, for example, GPS following, to screen and oversee reindeer crowds. This innovative variation improves the effectiveness of crowding rehearses while regarding the customary information went down through ages.

Furthermore, the Sámi have participated in backing and joint effort with administrative and global bodies to address the effects of environmental change and modern advancement on their reindeer grouping domains. The acknowledgment of their property privileges and the consideration of Sámi voices in dynamic cycles add to the progress of saving their special social legacy.

The Sámi story highlights the significance of mixing conventional insight with contemporary devices to explore the difficulties presented by ecological changes and outer tensions.

Maasai Mara Conservancies, Kenya:
Challenges Confronted:

The Maasai Mara in Kenya, eminent for its rich biodiversity and notorious natural life, confronted difficulties from environment discontinuity, poaching, and clashes among untamed life and nearby networks. The customary Maasai lifestyle, revolved around pastoralism, was likewise under tension because of evolving land-use designs.

Example of overcoming adversity:

The foundation of local area possessed conservancies in the Maasai Mara has been a groundbreaking achievement. By making associations between neighborhood Maasai people group and protection associations, these conservancies give an economical model to natural life preservation and local area improvement.

Income created through eco-the travel industry exercises, including safari stops and directed visits, is reinvested in protection endeavors and local area advancement projects. This supports the insurance of untamed life as well as upgrades the prosperity of the Maasai public.

The conservancy model has demonstrated successful in decreasing human-natural life clashes, as neighborhood networks become dynamic members in the protection venture. The outcome of Maasai Mara conservancies shows the potential for preservation drives that line up with the requirements and yearnings of native networks.

Incredible Green Wall Drive, Africa:
Challenges Confronted:

The Sahel district in Africa confronted serious difficulties, including desertification, land corruption, and food frailty. These difficulties were exacerbated by environmental change, prompting the removal of networks and loss of arable land.

Example of overcoming adversity:

The Incomparable Green Wall drive remains as a striking and aggressive reaction to the difficulties looked by the Sahel locale. Imagined as a skillet African exertion, the drive intends to battle desertification and land debasement by making a mosaic of green and useful scenes across the mainland.

Nations along the Sahel are effectively engaged with tree-establishing programs, reasonable land the board practices, and local area based projects. The Incomparable Green Wall tends to ecological difficulties as well as advances monetary open doors for neighborhood networks through agroforestry and reasonable horticulture.

The outcome of the Incomparable Green Wall lies in its cooperative and multi-layered approach, including legislatures, NGOs, and neighborhood networks. The drive outlines the groundbreaking effect of enormous scope natural undertakings that address both biological and financial difficulties.

Renewal of Native Dialects, Different Areas:

Challenges Confronted:

Native dialects all over the planet confronted the danger of elimination because of globalization, social osmosis, and the predominance of significant world dialects. The disintegration of semantic variety represented an immediate test to the transmission of social information and customs.

Example of overcoming adversity:

Endeavors to revive native dialects have arisen as examples of overcoming adversity in social safeguarding. Native people group, frequently in a joint effort with phonetic specialists and instructive establishments, have executed language renewal programs.

One such model is the rejuvenation of the Hawaiian language. Through instructive drives, drenching projects, and local area drove endeavors, the Hawaiian language has encountered a restoration. The outcome of these projects goes past phonetic conservation, adding to a more extensive social resurgence and a fortified feeling of character among the Hawaiian public.

Comparative drives are in progress in different districts, from the renewal of Maori in New Zealand to the endeavors to protect Local American dialects in the US. These victories feature the flexibility of networks focused on safeguarding their phonetic and social legacy.

Coordinated Water Asset The executives in Jordan:

Challenges Confronted:

Jordan, a water-scant nation, confronted difficulties of water shortage, over-extraction of groundwater, and the exhaustion of regular water sources. Fast populace development and expanded interest for water additionally exacerbated these difficulties.

Example of overcoming adversity:

Jordan's progress in coordinated water asset the board exhibits the positive effect of thorough procedures to address water difficulties. The nation carried out measures, for example, water reusing, water collecting, and the foundation of water client relationship to advance practical water use.

Moreover, mindfulness missions and local area commitment drives cultivated a culture of water preservation among the populace. The outcome of coordinated water asset the executives in Jordan fills in as a model for different districts confronting water shortage, underlining the significance of an all encompassing and comprehensive way to deal with water administration.

4.3 Lessons Learned and Adaptive Strategies

In the unique scenes of ecological protection and social conservation, the excursion is checked by victories as well as by the examples gained from difficulties experienced en route. As people group, associations, and people endeavor to safeguard biological systems, biodiversity, and social legacy, the capacity to adjust and advance becomes vital. In this investigation, we dig into the illustrations gained from snags confronted and the versatile systems utilized to explore intricacies in both ecological protection and social conservation.

1. **Embracing Flexibility Even with Environmental Change:**
   Examples Learned:
   The ubiquitous test of environmental change requests a nuanced comprehension of its effects on biological systems, networks, and social practices. Increasing temperatures, changed precipitation examples, and outrageous climate occasions present dangers to biodiversity and customary lifestyles. Illustrations gained from environmental change difficulties highlight the interconnectedness of ecological and social versatility.

   Versatile Systems:
   Versatile systems despite environmental change include a blend of logical experiences and conventional information. Coordinating environment science with native insight considers a comprehensive comprehension of the evolving climate. Drives, for example, environment brilliant farming, water protection, and economical land the board are versatile techniques that balance the conservation of social practices with the basic to relieve and adjust to environmental change.
   In the Maasai Mara conservancies of Kenya, for example, environment strong practices are coordinated into local area based protection endeavors. These incorporate economical touching practices, water asset the board, and differentiated work choices that engage nearby networks while upgrading the flexibility of environments.

2. **Adjusting Financial Turn of events and Social Conservation:**
   Examples Learned:
   The strain between monetary turn of events and social conservation is a repetitive subject in the stories of native networks and conventional social orders. The strain to adjust to present day monetary models can prompt the disintegration of social practices, dialects, and collective bonds. The examples learned highlight

the significance of finding some kind of harmony between monetary advancement and the protection of social legacy.

Versatile Systems:

Versatile systems in this setting include the investigation of maintainable monetary models that line up with social qualities. Local area based the travel industry, eco-accommodating endeavors, and mindful normal asset the board are instances of versatile techniques that produce pay while defending social personality.

In the Himalayan district of Ladakh, endeavors to offset financial advancement with social safeguarding have prompted the advancement of maintainable the travel industry. Local area drove drives center around exhibiting customary expressions, specialties, and celebrations, giving financial open doors to nearby occupants while safeguarding their interesting social practices.

3. **Cultivating Inclusivity in Protection Endeavors:**
   Illustrations Learned:

   By and large, protection endeavors have at times been condemned for dismissing the necessities and points of view of neighborhood networks, prompting clashes and opposition. Illustrations learned feature the significance of cultivating inclusivity and perceiving the organization of networks in the dynamic cycles connected with protection drives.

   Versatile Techniques:

   Versatile techniques that focus on inclusivity include connecting with neighborhood networks as dynamic members and partners in protection endeavors. This incorporates integrating conventional environmental information, regarding native administration structures, and guaranteeing that protection benefits are shared evenhandedly.

   The Incomparable Green Wall drive in Africa epitomizes a comprehensive methodology by including neighborhood networks in the rebuilding of corrupted scenes. By adjusting the objectives of biological rebuilding to the requirements of networks, the drive has effectively earned help and cooperation from those straightforwardly influenced by natural difficulties.

4. **Bridling Innovation for Protection and Social Conservation:**
   Illustrations Learned:

   The fast headway of innovation presents the two potential open doors and difficulties in the domains of protection and social safeguarding. Examples learned underscore the need to tackle mechanical advancements wisely, guaranteeing that they supplement as opposed to sabotage customary information and practices.

   Versatile Methodologies:

   Versatile methodologies include utilizing innovation as an instrument for strengthening instead of a power of disturbance. For instance, the utilization of geographic data frameworks (GIS), satellite symbolism, and versatile applications works with more viable checking of environments, untamed life, and social locales.

In the Amazon rainforest, native networks are using innovation to record and guide their conventional regions. This not just guides in that frame of mind of biodiversity-rich regions yet additionally builds up native land privileges. By consolidating conventional biological information with present day devices, networks improve their ability to shield both their social legacy and the regular habitat.

5. **Fortifying Culturally diverse Coordinated efforts:**
Illustrations Learned:

In a world described by expanding interconnectedness, culturally diverse joint efforts have become fundamental for tending to worldwide difficulties. Examples learned underline the significance of building spans between assorted social points of view, cultivating common regard, and recognizing the commitments of various networks to ecological protection and social conservation.

Versatile Techniques:

Versatile techniques include the foundation of cooperative structures that work with multifaceted trades and associations. Worldwide drives, joint exploration projects, and social trade programs make stages for sharing information and best practices.

The outcome of the cooperative endeavors in the Gorongosa Public Park in Mozambique represents the force of culturally diverse coordinated efforts. By uniting neighborhood networks, global associations, and government elements, the reclamation of the recreation area turned into a common vision. The versatile methodology of cooperative protection has renewed the biological system as well as fortified the social connections among networks and the land they occupy.

6. **Supporting Intergenerational Transmission of Information:**

Illustrations Learned:

The disintegration of customary information and social practices represents a critical danger to the coherence of native and conventional lifestyles. Illustrations learned stress the significance of supporting intergenerational transmission of information to guarantee the endurance of social legacy.

Versatile Methodologies:

Versatile methodologies include making roads for the exchange of information from elderly folks to more youthful ages. Social training programs, mentorship drives, and local area drove narrating projects are versatile systems that span generational holes and safeguard the insight implanted in conventional practices.

In Scandinavia, the Sámi public have carried out projects to guarantee the transmission of reindeer crowding information. Through apprenticeship models and instructive drives, youthful Sámi people get familiar with the complexities of crowding, route, and feasible land use from elderly folks, guaranteeing the coherence of this fundamental social practice.

Chapter 5

Zebra Warriors and Indigenous Communities

In the huge scenes of the African savannah, the Zebra Fighters stand as social gate-keepers, complicatedly associated with the land, natural life, and customs that have molded their character for a really long time. The Zebra Fighters, a native local area with a rich social legacy, epitomize the significant connection between native networks and the conditions they possess. In this investigation, we dig into the advantageous association between the Zebra Fighters and native networks at large, exploring how their social practices, ecological stewardship, and versatility add to the conservation of biodiversity and social lavishness.

1. **Social Personality and Customs of the Zebra Fighters:**
   Social Practices and Functions:
   The Zebra Heroes, with their unmistakable customs and practices, assume a urgent part in safeguarding their social personality. Vital to their lifestyle are functions, for example, the Dance of Stripes, a custom that mirrors the Zebra Champions' profound association with the regular rhythms of the savannah. This dance, described by perplexing developments and embellished clothing, represents the concordance between the local area and the land, commending the excellence of the zebra — an animal worshipped for its solidarity and elegance.

   The Zebra Heroes' social practices reach out past services to incorporate narrating, oral customs, and imaginative articulations that convey the local area's set of experiences, values, and relationship with the climate. These social components act as a living embroidery, winding around together the past, present, and eventual fate of the Zebra Heroes.

   Social Strength:
   The strength of the Zebra Fighters' social personality is clear in their capacity to adjust to changing conditions while safeguarding the center fundamentals

70

of their practices. As outside impacts and advancement infringe upon their domains, the Zebra Fighters effectively take part in social tact, supporting for the acknowledgment and security of their social practices.

The safeguarding of their language, moves, and ceremonies turns into a demonstration of social flexibility — a demonstration of their obligation to passing down the lavishness of their legacy to people in the future. The Zebra Fighters' story fills in as a motivation for native networks all around the world, featuring the significance of social pride and progression notwithstanding outer tensions.

2. **Native Information and Natural Stewardship:**
All encompassing Relationship with Nature:
Native people group, including the Zebra Fighters, frequently have a significant comprehension of their normal environmental elements. Their insight, procured through hundreds of years of close communication with the climate, incorporates unpredictable insights regarding environments, natural life conduct, and economical asset the board.

The Zebra Fighters' comprehensive relationship with nature is implanted in their regular routines. From following relocation examples to understanding the restorative properties of neighborhood plants, their native information shapes a far reaching structure for supportable conjunction with the savannah. This profound natural comprehension supports the Zebra Heroes as well as adds to the more extensive protection of the climate they call home.

Saving Biodiversity:
Native people group are many times the overseers of biodiversity-rich districts, and the Zebra Fighters are no special case. Their conventional land-use rehearses, educated by ages regarding perception and transformation, focus on the conservation of environments and natural life. The roaming way of life of the Zebra Champions, portrayed via occasional movements, limits the effect on any single region, permitting environments to recover and flourish.

Innate in their social practices is a pledge to keeping up with the fragile harmony between human requirements and the prosperity of the climate. The Zebra Fighters' job as stewards of the savannah positions them as central members in the preservation of biodiversity — an obligation woven into the texture of their social legacy.

Economical Land The board:
The Zebra Champions participate in supportable land the board rehearses that mirror their environmental insight. Conventional techniques for rotational munching, controlled consumes, and the aversion of overexploitation guarantee the flexibility of prairies and backing the variety of plant and creature life. These practices have been sharpened over hundreds of years, mirroring a significant comprehension of the interconnectedness of all living creatures inside the biological system.

As the worldwide local area wrestles with the results of impractical land use, the

Zebra Champions' methodology offers significant experiences into the agreeable concurrence between native networks and their surroundings. Their economical land the executives rehearses are a living illustration of how social practices can be a directing power in ecological protection.

3. **Difficulties to Native People group and Zebra Heroes:**
Living space Fracture and Misfortune:
One of the principal challenges looked by native networks, including the Zebra Fighters, is living space fracture and misfortune. Fast urbanization, agrarian extension, and foundation improvement infringe upon customary regions, upsetting transitory courses and decreasing the accessibility of assets.

For the Zebra Fighters, the outcomes of natural surroundings fracture reach out past environmental interruptions to social difficulties. The Dance of Stripes, well established in the normal rhythms of the savannah, turns into a representative articulation of the effect of environment misfortune on their conventional functions. The fracture of scenes represents a danger not exclusively to biodiversity yet additionally to the social practices indistinguishable from the land.

Outer Tensions and Modernization:
Native people group all over the planet, including the Zebra Heroes, face outer tensions driven by globalization, financial interests, and the impact of current ways of life. The charm of urbanization, formal schooling, and financial open doors outside customary settings represents a test to the continuation of native lifestyles.

The more youthful age of Zebra Champions wrestles with the strain between safeguarding social legacy and embracing outside impacts. As the elements of the savannah and cultural designs develop, the Zebra Champions should explore a sensitive equilibrium to guarantee the congruity of their customs notwithstanding modernization.

Environmental Change Effects:
The effects of environmental change, including eccentric weather conditions, delayed dry seasons, and changes in biological systems, present huge difficulties to native networks like the Zebra Champions. Changes in precipitation examples and temperatures influence the accessibility of water as well as the movement examples of natural life that the local area relies upon.

Adjusting to these environmental change influences requires native networks to rethink customary practices and foster creative methodologies for strength.

The Zebra Champions, personally associated with the regular patterns of the savannah, wind up exploring a scene going through significant movements, requiring versatile measures to support both their social practices and environmental equilibrium.

4. **Versatile Procedures and Arrangements:**
Local area Drove Preservation Drives:
Versatile procedures utilized by the Zebra Champions and native networks

worldwide frequently rotate around local area drove preservation drives. Perceiving the characteristic connection between social practices and ecological prosperity, these drives engage neighborhood networks to play a functioning job in protection endeavors.

On account of the Zebra Champions, people group drove preservation includes supportable land the executives, untamed life checking, and living space rebuilding. The Dance of Stripes, once emblematic exclusively of social legacy, presently entwines with preservation as the Zebra Heroes effectively participate in safeguarding the territories basic to the endurance of zebras and different species.

Integrating Customary Information into Protection:

The reconciliation of conventional information into protection rehearses is a key versatile technique utilized by native networks. For the Zebra Champions, this includes cooperating with preservation associations and legislative organizations to consolidate exceptionally old insight with present day logical methodologies. The Zebra Champions effectively partake in natural life observing, using their native information to follow creature developments and recognize indications of biological wellbeing. By overcoming any issues among conventional and logical information, the local area adds to more powerful and socially delicate protection rehearses.

Social Tact and Backing:

Social tact and backing arise as strong versatile techniques for native networks like the Zebra Fighters. Drawing in with outside substances, administrative bodies, and global associations permits these networks to enhance their voices and feature the significance of their social practices in keeping up with environmental equilibrium.

The Zebra Fighters effectively partake in backing endeavors to safeguard their conventional terrains and biodiversity. By outlining their social practices as fundamental to the wellbeing of the savannah, they participate in conciliatory talk that looks for acknowledgment and backing for their exceptional lifestyle.

Financial Broadening and Manageability:

Perceiving the financial tensions looked by native networks, versatile methodologies frequently incorporate monetary expansion and supportability measures. For the Zebra Heroes, this might include investigating elective vocations that line up with their social qualities while giving monetary steadiness.

Local area based the travel industry, manageable agribusiness, and eco-accommodating endeavors are instances of financial expansion that at the same time add to natural preservation. By utilizing their social legacy as a special selling point, the Zebra Champions set out monetary open doors that supplement their conventional lifestyle.

5. **Coordinated efforts with Preservation Associations:**
   Associations for Preservation:

Coordinated efforts with preservation associations and NGOs are instrumental in supporting the endeavors of native networks like the Zebra Fighters. These organizations unite the mastery of protectionists with the customary information on native networks, making a synergistic way to deal with natural safeguarding.

The Zebra Champions team up with protection associations to carry out ventures like territory rebuilding, against poaching drives, and local area based preservation programs. These joint efforts furnish the local area with admittance to assets, preparing, and worldwide organizations, supporting the interconnectedness of nearby and worldwide preservation endeavors.

Schooling and Limit Building:

Training and limit building arise as fundamental parts of cooperative endeavors between native networks and preservation associations. Enabling people group individuals with the abilities and information expected to effectively take part in protection cultivates a feeling of pride and supportability.

For the Zebra Champions, schooling drives might incorporate ecological stewardship programs, natural life checking preparing, and supportable land the board studios. By building the limit of local area individuals, preservation associations add to the drawn out versatility of both the local area and the biological systems they possess.

Comprehensive Dynamic Cycles:

Successful coordinated efforts focus on comprehensive dynamic cycles that regard the independence and organization of native networks. The Zebra Fighters effectively take part in the turn of events and execution of protection drives, guaranteeing that their points of view, values, and needs are necessary to the dynamic cycle.

Comprehensive dynamic encourages a feeling of pride as well as upgrades the viability of preservation procedures. By adjusting outside mediations to the needs of the Zebra Champions, these coordinated efforts make an establishment for manageable and socially delicate preservation rehearses.

6. **The Job of Worldwide Elements in Native Preservation:**

Worldwide Acknowledgment of Native Privileges:

At the worldwide level, the acknowledgment of native privileges has acquired unmistakable quality as a basic part of worldwide preservation endeavors. Structures like the Assembled Countries Announcement on the Privileges of Native People groups (UNDRIP) accentuate the significance of regarding and safeguarding the freedoms of native networks, including their entitlement to keep up with and fortify their particular social practices.

The Zebra Heroes, in the same way as other native networks, benefit from the developing affirmation of their freedoms on the worldwide stage. This acknowledgment approves their social legacy as well as supports the basic of remembering native points of view for global preservation plans.

Worldwide Financing and Backing:

Worldwide substances, including legislative bodies and non-legislative associations, assume a critical part in giving financing and backing to native preservation drives. The Zebra Fighters might get monetary help, specialized mastery, and promotion support from worldwide accomplices, reinforcing their ability to address natural difficulties.

The worldwide local area's obligation to biodiversity protection, environmental change moderation, and the safeguarding of social variety is reflected in the help stretched out to native networks. This cooperative methodology perceives that the difficulties looked by the Zebra Fighters are not secluded however are interconnected with worldwide endeavors to safeguard the planet's environmental and social variety.

Worldwide Stages for Native Voices:

Worldwide stages give roads to native networks to voice their interests, share their insight, and supporter for the conservation of their social and ecological legacy. The Zebra Heroes, through their support in worldwide conversations, add to the more extensive talk on native freedoms, ecological protection, and reasonable turn of events.

Worldwide stages additionally act as systems for trading best works on, encouraging diverse joint efforts, and affecting strategies that influence native networks. By enhancing their voices on the global stage, the Zebra Champions become influencers for their own local area as well as for native people groups around the world.

5.1 Collaborative Conservation with Indigenous Peoples

Cooperative protection with native people groups addresses a change in perspective in the way to deal with natural stewardship, perceiving the perplexing connection between social legacy and biodiversity. Native people group, frequently the overseers of environmentally rich scenes, assume a vital part in practical asset the board and the protection of extraordinary biological systems.

In this investigation, we dig into the standards, practices, difficulties, and achievements of cooperative preservation drives that include native people groups. By crossing over conventional information with contemporary preservation methodologies, these joint efforts prepare for a more all encompassing and compelling way to deal with safeguarding the planet's normal and social variety.

1. **Standards of Cooperative Preservation:**
   Regard for Native Information:

   A foundation of cooperative preservation is the regard and joining of native information into protection endeavors. Native people group, through ages of lived insight, have a profound comprehension of nearby biological systems, natural life conduct, and economical asset the board. This customary information is a significant supplement to logical methodologies, offering bits of knowledge that improve the viability and social responsiveness of preservation systems.

   Regarding native information includes perceiving the comprehensive idea of conventional natural comprehension, which frequently stretches out past absolutely logical classifications. The interaction between natural, social, and otherworldly aspects is fundamental to native viewpoints, enhancing protection tries with a more complete perspective.

Acknowledgment of Native Privileges:

Cooperative preservation is established in the acknowledgment and regard for the freedoms of native people groups. This incorporates the right to self-assurance, land freedoms, and the insurance of social practices. Worldwide systems, like the Unified Countries Statement on the Privileges of Native People groups (UNDRIP), stress the significance of getting the land and asset freedoms of native networks to guarantee their dynamic support and dynamic expert in protection endeavors.

By recognizing and maintaining native privileges, cooperative protection drives expect to redress verifiable treacheries, enable nearby networks, and cultivate a feeling of responsibility over the preservation interaction. This acknowledgment lays out an establishment for organizations in light of trust, common regard, and shared liability.

Inclusivity and Cooperation:

Inclusivity is a central rule of cooperative preservation, underscoring the dynamic support of native networks in dynamic cycles. Significant commitment guarantees that preservation drives line up with the needs, values, and yearnings of nearby networks. Comprehensive methodologies additionally perceive the assorted points of view inside native gatherings, advancing orientation value and the association of youth in protection endeavors.

The consideration of native voices in the preparation, execution, and assessment of preservation projects improves the social importance and long haul maintainability of drives. By cultivating associations based on neutral ground, cooperative protection attempts are bound to prevail with regards to accomplishing their natural and social targets.

Social Responsiveness and Versatility:

Social responsiveness is fundamental in cooperative preservation to explore the variety of native societies and customs. Protection systems should be versatile to the extraordinary settings, otherworldly convictions, and standard acts of every local area. This requires a continuous discourse, where preservation experts effectively pay attention to and gain from native accomplices.

Versatility is vital, as protection drives should develop in light of changes in biological systems, environment, and local area elements. The capacity to coordinate customary environmental information with contemporary logical bits of knowledge considers a stronger and responsive way to deal with protection challenges.

2. **Rehearses in Cooperative Protection:**

Local area Based Protection Models:

Local area based protection models enable native networks to play a focal job in dealing with their regular assets. These models frequently include the foundation of safeguarded regions, co-oversaw by neighborhood networks and preservation specialists. The Sámi nation in Scandinavia, for instance, effectively participate in reindeer grouping rehearses that add to the preservation of huge, biodiverse scenes.

Through people group based preservation, native networks become stewards of their domains, using customary information to execute maintainable land the board rehearses. Income produced from eco-the travel industry, manageable collecting, or different undertakings is frequently reinvested in preservation drives and local area improvement projects, making a pattern of shared benefit.

Native Drove Protection Drives:

Native drove preservation drives arise when networks freely assume responsibility for safeguarding their normal and social legacy. These drives are driven by a profound feeling of obligation and association with the land. The Gatekeepers of the Timberland in the Amazon rainforest, for example, are native local area individuals who effectively watch and safeguard their domains against unlawful logging and different dangers.

Native drove preservation projects frequently include a blend of customary practices and inventive methodologies.

The coordination of present day instruments, like GPS innovation and satellite symbolism, empowers native networks to screen and protect their regions all the more successfully while keeping up with the respectability of their social practices.

Incorporated Land Use Arranging:

Cooperative protection supports coordinated land use arranging that regards the interconnectedness of environments and social practices. Native land-use plans think about the occasional developments of untamed life, conventional hunting and assembling regions, and areas of otherworldly importance. This comprehensive methodology perceives that protection is certainly not a different undertaking however a necessary piece of supporting both biodiversity and social variety.

Coordinated land use arranging frequently includes associations with legislative bodies, protection associations, and exploration organizations. By integrating conventional information into land use strategies, these coordinated efforts advance more compelling and socially delicate ways to deal with natural administration.

Organizations with Native Information Holders:

Laying out organizations with native information holders is a critical practice in cooperative protection. These people, frequently elderly folks or local area pioneers, are vaults of customary environmental information went down through ages. Cooperative activities benefit from the experiences and direction of these information holders, guaranteeing that protection procedures line up with social qualities and needs.

The sharing of native information is a two-way process, cultivating common regard and learning. Native information holders add to logical comprehension, and thus, protection specialists offer help for the safeguarding and transmission of conventional information to more youthful ages.

3. **Challenges in Cooperative Protection:**
Verifiable Shameful acts and Doubt:

Verifiable shameful acts, including colonization and the constrained dislodging of native people groups, have left enduring scars that add to doubt in co-operative preservation endeavors. Numerous native networks have encountered the adverse consequences of remotely forced preservation measures, like the foundation of safeguarded regions without local area discussion.

Building trust requires a guarantee to tending to verifiable treacheries, perceiving previous slip-ups, and effectively including native networks in dynamic cycles. Cooperative preservation drives should focus on straightforward correspondence and regard for the independence of native accomplices to beat verifiable doubt.

Outside Tensions and Advancement:

Native domains frequently face outside pressures from ventures looking for admittance to normal assets, framework advancement, and the development of farming. These outside pressures represent a danger to both biodiversity and social legacy. The conflict between preservation objectives and monetary advancement can prompt struggles, as seen in areas where mining or logging interests converge with native grounds.

Exploring outside pressures requires a sensitive harmony among preservation and improvement targets. Cooperative methodologies ought to expect to find mutual benefit arrangements that help monetary improvement while regarding the privileges and needs of native networks. This requires discourse, exchange, and a guarantee to feasible improvement rehearses.

Environmental Change Effects:

The effects of environmental change, remembering shifts for atmospheric conditions, outrageous occasions, and modifications in biological systems, present huge difficulties to cooperative preservation endeavors. Native people group, frequently exceptionally receptive to changes in their surroundings, are encountering the outcomes of a quickly warming planet.

Adjusting to environmental change requires cooperative preservation drives to be adaptable and responsive. This might include the improvement of environment versatility techniques, the reconciliation of customary environment variation practices, and backing for native networks to adapt to the effects of an evolving environment.

Absence of Acknowledgment and Portrayal:

At times, native networks face an absence of acknowledgment and portrayal in dynamic cycles connected with preservation. This can bring about protection techniques that don't line up with the needs and viewpoints of neighborhood networks. The prohibition of native voices subverts the viability of cooperative preservation and sustains a hierarchical methodology.

Tending to the absence of acknowledgment and portrayal includes making stages for native pioneers, information holders, and local area individuals to take part in protection administration effectively. Drives that focus on inclusivity and regard for assorted points of view add to more evenhanded and effective protection results.

4. **Triumphs and Positive Results:**

Biodiversity Protection:

Cooperative protection drives with native people groups have exhibited positive results for biodiversity preservation. Native oversaw regions frequently harbor more elevated levels of biodiversity, as conventional land-use rehearses are lined up with environmental cycles.

The conjunction of native networks and untamed life, like the Maasai in East Africa and their cooperations with natural life, represents the potential for amicable connections among people and nature.

Research has shown that biodiversity areas of interest correspond with regions generally oversaw by native people groups. By perceiving the protection worth of native grounds, cooperative drives add to the safeguarding of interesting environments and the species they support.

Social Rejuvenation and Pride:

Cooperative protection adds to the rejuvenation and conservation of native societies. At the point when native information and practices are coordinated into protection endeavors, it encourages a feeling of social pride and character. The recovery of conventional functions, dialects, and expressions becomes interwoven with the preservation story, supporting that social legacy and ecological stewardship are interconnected.

In locales where cooperative protection is effective, native networks experience a resurgence of social practices. This reinforces local area union as well as fills in as a wellspring of motivation for other native gatherings trying to recover and praise their social legacy.

Monetary Strengthening and Practical Jobs:

Cooperative protection models frequently enable native networks financially by giving practical job amazing open doors. Through drives like local area based the travel industry, feasible gathering of non-wood timberland items, or eco-accommodating undertakings, native networks create pay while keeping up with their association with the land.

Financial strengthening adds to the self-assurance of native networks and decrease reliance on exercises that might hurt the climate. By adjusting preservation to feasible jobs, cooperative drives make a pathway for native networks to flourish financially without undermining their social and environmental honesty.

Improved Administration and Independence:

Fruitful cooperative protection drives add to upgraded administration and independence for native networks. Participatory dynamic cycles, where native pioneers effectively shape protection methodologies, reinforce the self-administration of native regions. This strengthening cultivates a feeling of pride over protection drives and positions native networks as key entertainers in ecological administration.

In locales where cooperative protection has succeeded, native administration structures frequently assume a focal part in overseeing normal assets.

This acknowledgment of independence adds to the drawn out supportability of protection endeavors and lines up with the standards of self-assurance illustrated in global systems.

5. **Future Headings in Cooperative Preservation:**

Reinforcing Lawful Securities:

One future course in cooperative preservation includes reinforcing lawful securities for native privileges and regions. This incorporates the proper acknowledgment of native land residency, the foundation of components free of charge, earlier, and informed assent (FPIC), and the fuse of native overall sets of laws into public legitimate structures.

By supporting legitimate securities, cooperative protection drives can give a safer establishment to the dynamic contribution of native networks in dynamic cycles. This legitimate acknowledgment supports the standards of regard, inclusivity, and independence that support effective cooperative endeavors.

Putting resources into Native Schooling and Limit Building:

Putting resources into training and limit working inside native networks is vital for the progress of cooperative preservation. By giving preparation in protection science, feasible asset the board, and backing, native local area individuals can effectively partake in and lead preservation drives.

Instruction projects ought to be planned cooperatively, consolidating both conventional information and contemporary logical methodologies. The objective is to construct a framework of talented people inside native networks who can really add to preservation endeavors while safeguarding their social legacy.

Advancing Diverse Coordinated efforts:

Advancing diverse coordinated efforts includes making stages for the trading of information and encounters among native and non-native networks. By cultivating understanding and shared regard, these joint efforts add to the advancement of inventive and comprehensive protection draws near.

Worldwide organizations that span assorted social viewpoints, like the trading of native information between networks from various locales, give potential chances to shared learning. Multifaceted joint efforts likewise add to the worldwide talk on protection, recognizing the interconnectedness of social and biological variety.

Increasing Fruitful Models:

Recognizing and increasing effective cooperative preservation models is fundamental for far reaching influence. Projects that have shown positive results regarding biodiversity preservation, social renewal, and monetary strengthening can act as motivations for comparable drives in different locales.

Increasing fruitful models includes repeating powerful systems as well as adjusting them to nearby settings. Perceiving the variety of native societies and environments, cooperative protection drives ought to be customized to the particular requirements and desires of every local area.

5.2 Respecting Traditional Knowledge and Practices

Regarding customary information and practices is a principal principle in encouraging social responsiveness, manageability, and cooperative connections. Native people group, frequently the overseers old enough old insight, have an abundance of experiences into economical asset the board, natural elements, and social legacy. Regarding this customary information includes recognizing its comprehensive nature, incorporating ecological viewpoints as well as profound, social, and social aspects.

Customary practices, whether in farming, land stewardship, or biodiversity preservation, are profoundly entwined with the social texture of native social orders. These practices have developed over ages, addressing a significant comprehension of the normal world. Perceiving and regarding these practices isn't just a token of regard yet in addition a logical way to deal with tending to contemporary difficulties.

In cooperative protection, the coordination of conventional information improves and refines preservation procedures, making them more compelling and socially applicable. Regarding conventional information isn't only a social thought yet an acknowledgment that supportable arrangements rise out of a union of customary thinking and contemporary science. In doing as such, we safeguard the legacy of native networks as well as manufacture pathways to a more agreeable concurrence among humankind and the climate.

5.3 Building Sustainable Partnerships

Practical organizations are the foundation of viable and enduring drives, particularly in domains like protection, social turn of events, and social conservation. Whether between non-benefit associations, legislative bodies, or networks, the rules that support these joint efforts are fundamental for making significant, fair, and getting through change.

1. **Shared Vision and Objectives:**

   The underpinning of any manageable organization lies in a common vision and shared objectives. Adjusting the goals of all elaborate gatherings guarantees a bound together bearing and an aggregate obligation to the ideal results. This common vision turns into the directing power that ties accomplices together, cultivating a feeling of direction and union. In cooperative endeavors like protection undertakings or local area improvement drives, a mutual perspective of the ideal effect makes a guide for aggregate activity.

2. **Shared Regard and Acknowledgment:**
   Regard is a cash that fills practical organizations. Perceiving the special qualities, viewpoints, and commitments of each accomplice constructs an underpinning of trust and collaboration. This rule is particularly significant in joint efforts including native networks, where recognizing conventional information, social practices, and privileges is fundamental to the progress of the organization. A conscious methodology guarantees that all accomplices feel esteemed, encouraging a climate where different voices are heard and appreciated.

3. **Comprehensive Independent direction:**
   Inclusivity is a vital principle of manageability in organizations. Dynamic cycles that include all partners, particularly those straightforwardly impacted by the drives, lead to additional hearty and persevering through results. This inclusivity reaches out past conventional exchanges to embrace local area commitment, guaranteeing that individuals most influenced have a veritable and powerful job in molding the bearing of the organization. In people group based projects, engaging neighborhood voices isn't simply a guideline; it is a pathway to manageable arrangements well established in the necessities and yearnings of the local area.

4. **Straightforward Correspondence:**
   Open and straightforward correspondence is the backbone of maintainable associations. Normal and genuine exchange guarantees that all accomplices are very much educated, cultivating trust and forestalling mistaken assumptions. Clear correspondence channels additionally take into consideration the successful sharing of data, assets, and illustrations learned. Straightforwardness fabricates responsibility, a basic component in supporting organizations over the long haul. Whether tending to difficulties or praising victories, keeping up with clear and open lines of correspondence is essential for the strength of the cooperation.

5. **Limit Building and Strengthening:**
   Reasonable organizations focus on the structure of limits inside each accomplice, advancing strengthening and versatility. This includes sharing information and abilities as well as putting resources into the capacities of people and networks. In preservation associations, for instance, limit building might envelop preparing neighborhood networks in maintainable land the board practices or outfitting them with the devices to effectively take part in natural life checking.

The objective is to make independent and enabled accomplices equipped for driving positive change autonomously.

6. **Adaptability and Flexibility:**

The capacity to adjust and develop is a sign of feasible organizations. In powerful conditions, whether affected by moving social elements, financial changes, or biological varieties, accomplices should be coordinated and responsive. Adaptability permits organizations to explore difficulties, gain from encounters, and change procedures depending on the situation. This flexibility guarantees that the joint effort stays applicable and powerful all through its length, even notwithstanding unexpected conditions.

7. **Shared Assets and Obligations:**

Maintainability in organizations includes a fair conveyance of the two assets and obligations. Accomplices should contribute fairly to the cooperative exertion, be it regarding financing, mastery, or on-the-ground endeavors. This common obligation encourages a feeling of responsibility and responsibility, keeping any single accomplice from bearing an excessive weight. Impartial asset dispersion guarantees that the organization can weather conditions provokes and keeps on flourishing.

8. **Observing and Assessment:**

Standard checking and assessment components are fundamental to manageability. Organizations benefit from continuous appraisals of progress, effect, and difficulties. This iterative cycle permits accomplices to refine methodologies, commend victories, and address regions that might require changes. Observing and assessment not just add to the improvement of the joint effort yet in addition act as a reason for responsibility to partners, funders, and the networks in question.

9. **Long haul Vision and Heritage:**

Feasible organizations expand their look past prompt objectives, imagining a drawn out effect and heritage. This expects accomplices to think about the persevering through impacts of their joint effort on the networks, conditions, or issues they look to address. In social conservation drives, for example, a drawn out vision might include procedures for passing down customary information to people in the future.

An emphasis on inheritance guarantees that the organization's effect rises above its nearby length, leaving a positive engraving on the networks and environments included.

10. **Festivity of Accomplishments:**

Commending accomplishments, both of all shapes and sizes, is necessary to supporting organizations. Recognizing achievements cultivates a feeling of achievement, propels accomplices, and supports the cooperative soul. In protection organizations, for instance, praising the recuperation of a compromised animal categories or the effective execution of an economical practice gathers speed for proceeded with endeavors. Perceiving accomplishments adds to the general positive environment of the organization, rousing continuous responsibility and commitment.

Chapter 6

Global Impact and Recognition

In the domain of cooperative preservation and native organizations, the worldwide effect is a demonstration of the extraordinary force of bound together endeavors. As people group, associations, and countries meet up to address squeezing natural and social difficulties, the reverberation of their undertakings reaches out a long ways past neighborhood borders. This investigation digs into the significant worldwide effect and acknowledgment accumulated by drives that focus on cooperation, inclusivity, and the combination of native information. From biodiversity protection to social conservation, these endeavors not just shape the fate of the locales they straight-forwardly impact yet additionally add to a worldwide story of interconnectedness and shared liability.

1. **Biodiversity Preservation on a Worldwide Scale:**
   The Cornerstone Job of Native Terrains:
   Cooperative preservation drives with native people groups significantly affect worldwide biodiversity. Native terrains, frequently wealthy in exceptional environments and biodiversity areas of interest, go about as cornerstones in the worldwide work to safeguard Earth's natural variety. The stewardship practices of native networks, established in customary information, add to the support of flawless and working biological systems.

   Research reliably exhibits that regions oversaw by native people groups will generally hold onto more significant levels of biodiversity. The complex comprehension of nearby biological systems permits native networks to take on supportable practices that fit with the normal world. By perceiving and supporting these practices, cooperative protection endeavors add to the conservation of worldwide biodiversity.

   Worldwide Meaning of Native Preservation Practices:
   The worldwide meaning of native preservation rehearses lies in their capacity to

offer elective models of feasible asset the executives. As the world wrestles with the difficulties of environmental change, deforestation, and loss of biodiversity, the practices created and refined by native networks over hundreds of years arise as signals of flexibility and versatility.

Native ways to deal with preservation frequently underline the interconnectedness of every living being and the significance of keeping up with environmental equilibrium. These standards line up with more extensive worldwide objectives of manageability and strength, making native information a significant wellspring of motivation for standard protection systems.

Commitments to Environmental Change Alleviation:

Cooperative protection drives that include native networks assume a critical part in environmental change relief. The assurance and reasonable administration of timberlands by native people groups add to the sequestration of carbon dioxide, assisting with alleviating the effects of environmental change. Timberlands oversaw by native networks act as carbon sinks, engrossing and putting away critical measures of carbon from the environment.

Perceiving the job of native grounds in environmental change moderation has gotten forward movement on the worldwide stage. Worldwide structures, like the Paris Understanding, progressively recognize the significance of remembering native points of view and practices for systems for decreasing ozone harming substance emanations and improving carbon sequestration.

2. **Social Legacy Protection and Worldwide Acknowledgment:**

The Social Woven artwork of Native Variety:

Cooperative drives zeroed in on the protection of native social legacy add to the worldwide acknowledgment of the lavishness and variety of human societies. Native people group address a mosaic of dialects, customs, fine arts, and profound convictions that all in all structure a social embroidery. The conservation of this variety isn't just a moral objective yet additionally a wellspring of worldwide enhancement.

Even with globalization and social homogenization, the acknowledgment and festivity of native societies become demonstrations of flexibility. Native dialects, frequently archives of one of a kind information and approaches to grasping the world, add to the worldwide etymological variety. Endeavors to rejuvenate and support these dialects reverberate past neighborhood networks, cultivating a worldwide appreciation for the complex magnificence of human articulation.

Difficulties to Native Social Legacy:

Worldwide acknowledgment of the significance of saving native social legacy is increased by the difficulties these networks face. Fast cultural changes, infringement on customary grounds, and the disintegration of social practices present critical dangers to native societies. Cooperative drives that address these difficulties not just add to the prosperity of native networks yet in addition highlight the widespread worth of social variety.

The deficiency of native dialects, customary information, and social practices addresses a worldwide misfortune for mankind in general. Perceiving this, global associations and social establishments progressively underscore the significance of protecting native social legacy as a component of the more extensive work to advance social variety and inclusivity.

Advancing Intercultural Understanding:

Endeavors to protect native social legacy frequently remain inseparable with drives that advance intercultural understanding. By sharing stories, craftsmanship, and customs, native networks become ministers of social variety. The worldwide acknowledgment of native societies adds to a more nuanced and comprehensive comprehension of mankind's set of experiences and character.

Cooperative protection drives that incorporate social safeguarding into their structures make spaces for discourse and trade. This trade expands between native networks and outside accomplices as well as among different worldwide crowds. The narratives of versatility, variation, and social pride become spans that interface individuals across geological and social partitions.

3. **Acknowledgment of Native Privileges on the Worldwide Stage:**

Progressing Native Freedoms:

Cooperative protection drives play had a critical impact in propelling the acknowledgment of native privileges at the worldwide level. By and large, native networks have confronted underestimation, dispossession, and the infringement of their freedoms. In any case, the cooperative way to deal with protection stresses the standards of regard, inclusivity, and acknowledgment of native power.

Worldwide structures, like the Unified Countries Statement on the Freedoms of Native People groups (UNDRIP), typify a worldwide obligation to maintaining the privileges of native people groups. Cooperative protection endeavors add to the execution of these freedoms by guaranteeing that native networks have a voice in choices that influence their properties, assets, and lifestyles.

Free, Earlier, and Informed Assent (FPIC):

The idea of Free, Earlier, and Informed Assent (FPIC) is a urgent component of perceiving and regarding native privileges in cooperative protection. FPIC recognizes the right of native networks to give or keep their agree to projects that might influence them. This rule guarantees that choices are made in counsel with, and with the assent of, the impacted networks.

The joining of FPIC in cooperative preservation rehearses sets a norm for moral commitment with native people groups. It stresses the significance of veritable organization, straightforward correspondence, and a pledge to the independence of native networks in choices connected with natural administration and protection.

Worldwide Fortitude for Native Freedoms:

The worldwide effect of cooperative protection is apparent in the developing fortitude for native privileges. Backing endeavors, drove by both native networks and their partners, cause to notice issues, for example, land privileges, social safeguarding, and the right to self-assurance. Social developments and world-wide missions enhance the voices of native pioneers, looking for equity and acknowledgment on the worldwide stage.

Worldwide fortitude for native privileges isn't restricted to manner of speaking; it converts into substantial activities. Protection associations, states, and world-wide bodies progressively incorporate native viewpoints into approaches, tasks, and systems. This acknowledgment reaches out past protection drives, impact-ing more extensive conversations on basic freedoms, civil rights, and reasonable turn of events.

4. **Logical Cooperation and Information Trade:**
   Incorporation of Customary and Logical Information:
   Cooperative preservation drives work with the reconciliation of customary na-tive information with contemporary logical methodologies. This combination of bits of knowledge upgrades the general viability of protection techniques. Native people group, with their profound comprehension of nearby biological systems, contribute important data on biodiversity, occasional examples, and the interconnectedness of species.

   Logical joint effort perceives that both customary and logical information are fundamental parts of a thorough way to deal with ecological stewardship. Native information, frequently gathered over ages, supplements logical information by giving setting, subtlety, and a comprehensive comprehension of biological elements.

   Enabling Native Researchers:
   The worldwide effect of cooperative protection is additionally obvious in the strengthening of native researchers and scientists. By cultivating associations between native information holders and researchers, drives add to the limit working of native networks in logical techniques and exploration rehearses.

   Native researchers carry novel points of view and bits of knowledge to the worldwide academic local area. Their examination contributes not exclusively to neighborhood preservation endeavors yet additionally to the progression of logical information all the more comprehensively. Perceiving and enhancing the commitments of native researchers reinforces the worldwide academic local area's capacity to address complex ecological difficulties.

   Protecting Conventional Biological Information:
   Cooperative protection attempts effectively add to the conservation of con-ventional biological information (TEK). TEK incorporates the insight held by native networks with respect to the connections between living creatures, biological systems, and the climate. This information, went down through oral customs, is an important asset for grasping biological cycles.

   Saving TEK isn't just an issue of social legacy yet in addition a worldwide objective. As biological systems face exceptional difficulties, the experiences implanted in conventional natural information become progressively applicable. Cooperative drives that record, regard, and coordinate TEK into preservation rehearses add to a more extensive comprehension of supportable asset the board.

5. **Difficulties and Valuable open doors on the Worldwide Stage:**
Difficulties to Worldwide Acknowledgment:
Notwithstanding the positive effect, cooperative protection and native associations face difficulties on the worldwide stage. One huge test is the industriousness of generalizations and confusions about native people groups. Biased sees that cast native networks as impediments to improvement or as relics of the past can upset the acknowledgment of their fundamental job in preservation and reasonable turn of events.

Tending to these misguided judgments requires deliberate endeavors in training, backing, and narrating. By intensifying the tales of fruitful cooperative drives, scattering generalizations, and displaying the commitments of native networks, worldwide stories can move towards an additional exact and conscious comprehension.

Globalization and Outside Tensions:
The course of globalization, while interfacing different networks, likewise carries outer tensions to native domains. The infringement of worldwide ventures, extraction exercises, and improvement tasks can subvert nearby preservation endeavors. Adjusting the advantages of globalization with the need to safeguard native grounds and societies stays a complicated test.

Cooperative protection drives should explore these outer tensions by supporting for approaches that focus on natural maintainability and regard for native freedoms. Worldwide associations, incorporating those with non-legislative associations (NGOs) and global bodies, assume an essential part in supporting native networks in their endeavors to oppose outside pressures.

Open doors for Worldwide Backing:
The worldwide stage additionally offers amazing open doors for support and mindfulness building. Cooperative protection drives can use worldwide stages to cause to notice basic issues, prepare backing, and impact strategy changes.

Native pioneers and supporters progressively take part in worldwide gatherings, welcoming their points of view to conversations on environmental change, biodiversity protection, and maintainable turn of events.

Valuable open doors for worldwide backing incorporate drawing in with global bodies, taking part in meetings and occasions, and using computerized stages to enhance native voices. By outlining protection as a common worldwide obligation, cooperative drives add to a more extensive story that underscores the interconnectedness surprisingly and the planet.

6. **Contextual analyses in Worldwide Effect:**

The Amazon Rainforest and Native Watchmen:

The Amazon rainforest remains as a worldwide image of biodiversity and environmental significance. Cooperative preservation endeavors including native gatekeepers feature the potential for positive worldwide effect. Native people group in the Amazon, like the Gatekeepers of the Woodland, effectively watch and safeguard their domains against unlawful logging, mining, and different dangers.

The acknowledgment of the crucial pretended by native gatekeepers in defending the Amazon has collected global help. NGOs, legislatures, and worldwide natural associations progressively recognize the commitment of these watchmen to biodiversity protection and environmental change relief. The worldwide effect is apparent in missions, narratives, and promotion endeavors that feature the interconnectedness of the Amazon with worldwide environment designs.

Maasai Mara and Local area Based Preservation:

In East Africa, the Maasai Mara fills in as a great representation of local area based protection with worldwide ramifications. The Maasai people group, customarily pastoralists, has embraced protection rehearses that exist together with untamed life. Cooperative endeavors with preservation associations and legislative bodies have prompted the foundation of local area possessed conservancies.

The outcome of local area based protection in the Maasai Mara has drawn in worldwide consideration. The travel industry drives, frequently oversaw by neighborhood networks, add to both financial strengthening and natural life protection. The worldwide effect is clear in the advancement of supportable the travel industry models propelled by the Maasai Mara, impacting protection methodologies in different locales.

Acknowledgment of Native Freedoms in Canada:

In Canada, cooperative endeavors between native networks and the public authority have prompted critical steps in the acknowledgment of native freedoms. Milestone lawful cases, like the Delgamuukw and Tsilhqot'in choices, avow native land title and the obligation to counsel and oblige native people groups in asset advancement projects.

The worldwide effect of these lawful triumphs stretches out past Canada. They set trends for perceiving native privileges in different regions of the planet, impacting conversations ashore residency, self-assurance, and the security of customary domains. Native legitimate triumphs in Canada resound with worldwide developments upholding for equity, value, and the privileges of minimized networks.

6.1 Zebra Warriors on the Global Stage

The development of Zebra Champions on the worldwide stage addresses a dynamic and groundbreaking power in the domain of preservation. These committed people, propelled by the interconnectedness of mankind and nature, have fashioned a development that rises above boundaries, societies, and conventional preservation standards. This investigation dives into the worldwide effect of Zebra Heroes, their backing endeavors, and the persevering through engrave they are making on the shared mindset of preservation on a planetary scale.

1. **The Beginning of Zebra Heroes:**
   Zebra Heroes, as an idea and development, follows its underlying foundations to a promise to all encompassing and comprehensive protection. The expression "Zebra" epitomizes the possibility that preservation is certainly not a high contrast issue however a dynamic range of interconnected components. The beginning of Zebra Heroes lies in perceiving the requirement for different viewpoints, joint effort, and a takeoff from one-size-fits-all protection draws near.

   The development perceives that viable protection requires embracing the intricacy of natural frameworks and human associations. Zebra Champions reject the thought of a polarity among improvement and ecological stewardship, supporting for arrangements that orchestrate with both human requirements and the regular world.

2. **Standards and Targets of Zebra Fighters:**
   At its center, the Zebra Heroes development is directed by a bunch of standards and targets that recognize it as a remarkable power in the preservation scene.

   Comprehensive Preservation:
   Zebra Fighters champion the idea of all encompassing preservation, recognizing that ecological security is indivisible from social, social, and monetary contemplations. This comprehensive methodology perceives the relationship of environments and human prosperity, underscoring the significance of offsetting preservation objectives with the requirements of nearby networks.

   Inclusivity and Variety:
   Inclusivity and variety are principal principles of the Zebra Champions development. Perceiving the wealth of points of view that assorted societies bring to preservation, Zebra Heroes effectively try to incorporate voices customarily minimized in protection talk. This inclusivity stretches out to orientation, native information, and neighborhood networks, guaranteeing that the development mirrors the variety of the worldwide populace.

   Versatile Techniques:
   Zebra Fighters embrace versatile procedures that answer the powerful idea of natural difficulties. Perceiving that protection is definitely not a static undertaking, the development focuses on adaptability and advancement. This flexibility permits Zebra Champions to explore complex issues, incorporate new information, and answer really to arising dangers to biodiversity.

   Worldwide Joint effort:
   A characterizing component of Zebra Fighters is their obligation to worldwide cooperation. The development rises above geological limits, cultivating associations with associations, networks, and people all over the planet. This worldwide joint effort use shared skill, assets, and experiences to address protection challenges that reach out past the domain of any single district.

3. **Zebra Heroes in real life:**
   Zebra Heroes are effectively participated in on-the-ground protection drives,

strategy support, and mindfulness crusades that reverberate all around the world. Their effect is apparent in different circles, showing the broadness and profundity of their obligation to making positive change.

Safeguarding Imperiled Species:

Zebra Champions are at the front of endeavors to safeguard imperiled species. Whether battling poaching, supporting territory reclamation, or executing local area based preservation programs, Zebra Champions perceive the desperation of protecting biodiversity. The worldwide meaning of their work is obvious in the assurance of notable species that are imperative to the wellbeing of environments around the world.

Environment Rebuilding Drives:

Zebra Heroes lead territory reclamation drives that reach out past individual activities to address the bigger biological picture. By reestablishing corrupted scenes, fighting deforestation, and advancing feasible land-use rehearses, they add to the worldwide work to moderate environmental change and safeguard basic biological systems.

Local area Based Preservation Projects:

Perceiving the advantageous connection between neighborhood networks and preservation achievement, Zebra Heroes champion local area based protection programs. These drives enable networks to become stewards of their regular assets, adjusting protection objectives to the prosperity of the individuals who possess these scenes. The worldwide effect is obvious in the replication of fruitful models across assorted districts.

Coordinated efforts with Nearby and Worldwide Substances:

Zebra Heroes effectively look for coordinated efforts with nearby and global elements, manufacturing partnerships that intensify the effect of their preservation endeavors. By banding together with legislatures, non-benefit associations, scholastic establishments, and nearby networks, they make a trap of interconnected drives that address protection challenges from numerous points.

Utilization of Innovation in Preservation Endeavors:

Embracing the force of innovation, Zebra Heroes influence imaginative instruments for protection observing, information investigation, and public commitment. From satellite following of untamed life to the utilization of man-made consciousness in natural exploration, Zebra Champions bridle the capability of state of the art innovation to improve the proficiency and viability of protection drives on a worldwide scale.

4. **Establishing Standards and Targets:**

The establishing standards and targets of Zebra Champions act as the directing light for the development's worldwide undertakings.

Comprehensive Preservation Vision:

At the center of Zebra Heroes' establishing standards is an all encompassing protection vision that rises above customary limits. The development rejects compartmentalized approaches, perceiving that genuine protection achievement requires tending to interconnected difficulties couple. By embracing the intricacy of environments and the unpredictable snare of human instinct collaborations, Zebra Heroes advocate for techniques that think about biological, social, and social aspects.

Inclusivity and Variety as Qualities:
Zebra Fighters perceive inclusivity and variety as qualities that fuel viable preservation. By embracing a large number of points of view, information frameworks, and social bits of knowledge, the development improves how its might interpret complex protection issues.

Inclusivity stretches out not exclusively to human networks yet additionally to the assorted cluster of species and biological systems that structure the woven artwork of life on The planet.

Versatile Procedures for Strength:
Versatility is a foundation of Zebra Fighters' establishing standards. Understanding that preservation challenges are liquid and dynamic, the development focuses on versatile methodologies. This versatility empowers Zebra Fighters to explore unanticipated snags, gain from encounters, and consistently develop because of the changing scene of preservation.

Worldwide Coordinated effort for Aggregate Effect:
Zebra Champions imagine an existence where worldwide coordinated effort is the standard as opposed to the exemption. The development effectively looks for associations with people, associations, and legislatures around the world. By cultivating a feeling of shared liability regarding the planet, Zebra Champions intend to make a gradually expanding influence that rises above geological lines and makes an aggregate effect on a worldwide scale.

5. **Zebra Fighters and Native People group:**
An unmistakable part of Zebra Fighters' worldwide effect is their obligation to teaming up with and enabling native networks.

Regarding Conventional Information and Practices:
Zebra Champions perceive the priceless commitment of customary information and practices held by native networks. By regarding and incorporating this information into protection procedures, the development encourages a commonly useful relationship. This regard for conventional natural insight upgrades the adequacy of protection drives as well as adds to the safeguarding of social legacy.

Cooperative Protection with Native People groups:
Zebra Fighters effectively take part in cooperative preservation with native people groups, perceiving their job as caretakers of tremendous and biodiverse domains. This joint effort goes past tokenistic motions, holding back nothing that regard native privileges, focus on nearby independence, and consolidate conventional ways to deal with land the board. The worldwide effect is significant, as fruitful models of cooperative preservation with native networks rouse

comparable drives internationally.

Examples of overcoming adversity In spite of Difficulties:

Zebra Fighters celebrate examples of overcoming adversity that rise out of co-operative endeavors with native networks. Notwithstanding confronting verifiable shameful acts, land dispossession, and fundamental difficulties, native drove preservation drives upheld by Zebra Heroes feature the versatility and viability of these organizations. The worldwide meaning of these examples of overcoming adversity lies in their capability to motivate comparative joint efforts around the world.

Examples Learned and Versatile Systems:

The worldwide effect of Zebra Heroes isn't without its difficulties, and the development effectively gains from misfortunes and adjusts its systems likewise.

Challenges Looked by Zebra Heroes:

Zebra Heroes explore difficulties on numerous fronts, including protection from change, settled in interests in extractive ventures, and the worldwide ramifications of environmental change. The development defies confusions about the job of native networks in preservation, pushing for a change in perspective that perceives their fundamental commitments. Defeating these difficulties requires industriousness, vital coalitions, and a pledge to long haul influence.

Examples of overcoming adversity In spite of Difficulties:

Zebra Champions celebrate examples of overcoming adversity that rise up out of cooperative endeavors with native networks. In spite of confronting authentic treacheries, land dispossession, and foundational challenges, native drove protection drives upheld by Zebra Fighters feature the strength and viability of these organizations. The worldwide meaning of these examples of overcoming adversity lies in their capability to motivate comparable coordinated efforts around the world.

Illustrations Learned and Versatile Methodologies:

The worldwide effect of Zebra Champions isn't without its difficulties, and the development effectively gains from misfortunes and adjusts its methodologies as needs be.

Impediments Looked by Zebra Heroes:

Zebra Champions experience deterrents, for example, protection from change, settled in interests in extractive enterprises, and the worldwide ramifications of environmental change. The development stands up to misguided judgments about the job of native networks in preservation, supporting for a change in outlook that perceives their imperative commitments. Defeating these difficulties requires perseverance, vital coalitions, and a guarantee to long haul influence.

Examples of overcoming adversity In spite of Difficulties:

Zebra Fighters celebrate examples of overcoming adversity that rise up out of cooperative endeavors with native networks. Notwithstanding confronting authentic treacheries, land dispossession, and fundamental difficulties, native drove protection drives upheld by Zebra Champions exhibit the flexibility and adequacy of these associations. The worldwide meaning of these examples of overcoming adversity lies in their capability to rouse comparable coordinated efforts around the world.

Examples Learned and Versatile Methodologies:
Zebra Champions approach difficulties as any open doors for development, learning important examples that shape their versatile methodologies. The development perceives the requirement for adaptability even with dynamic ecological and social scenes. By constantly rethinking and refining their methodologies, Zebra Champions show a promise to flexibility and a steady commitment to the standards of all encompassing preservation.

6. **Worldwide Effect and Acknowledgment:**

The worldwide effect and acknowledgment of Zebra Fighters reach out past preservation victories to impact global stories and arrangements.

Acknowledgment on the Worldwide Stage:
Zebra Heroes have gathered acknowledgment on the global stage, affecting conversations on biodiversity protection, environmental change moderation, and reasonable turn of events. Their promotion endeavors reverberate in worldwide discussions, molding strategies that focus on inclusivity, regard for native freedoms, and comprehensive ways to deal with ecological difficulties.

Rousing Worldwide Developments:
The worldwide effect of Zebra Heroes lies in their capacity to motivate developments past the domain of conventional protection. Their standards of inclusivity, versatility, and worldwide coordinated effort act as an outline for addressing more extensive difficulties connected with civil rights, common liberties, and the interconnectedness of worldwide issues. Zebra Champions are not restricted to preservation; they are impetuses for fundamental change on a planetary scale.

Tradition of Zebra Fighters:
As Zebra Fighters proceed with their excursion, their heritage is flourishing in the shared perspective of a worldwide local area focused on an additional manageable and agreeable future.

The development's effect stretches out past individual activities or triumphs, leaving a getting through engrave on the manner in which mankind sees its relationship with the normal world.

6.2 Awards and Accolades
Grants and honors are strong affirmations that perceive and celebrate extraordinary commitments, accomplishments, and effect in different fields. In the domain of protection and natural stewardship, people and associations that show exceptional responsibility frequently get lofty honors, cementing their remaining as pioneers in the

worldwide development. These awards honor the beneficiaries as well as act as signals, directing others to imitate their commitment and achievement.

Acknowledgment for Protection Greatness:

Grants and awards in the field of preservation commonly honor people, associations, or ventures that have exhibited greatness in safeguarding biodiversity, advancing economical practices, and encouraging local area commitment. These acknowledgments frequently feature imaginative methodologies, effective protection results, and a commitment to the standards of all encompassing ecological stewardship.

Global Preservation Grants:

On the worldwide stage, prestigious honors, for example, the Goldman Ecological Award, the Whitley Grants, and the Future for Nature Grants focus on people and grassroots associations making huge commitments to protection. These honors lift the beneficiaries to a place of impact, giving a stage to enhance their voices, share their encounters, and motivate others to join the worldwide work to safeguard the planet.

Acknowledgment of Native Administration:

Grants likewise assume an essential part in recognizing the commitments of native pioneers and networks to preservation. Given their remarkable information on environments and conventional manageable practices, native people frequently get honors perceiving their imperative job in saving biodiversity and keeping up with the harmony among people and nature.

Logical Acknowledgment in Protection Exploration:

In the logical domain, grants honor analysts and foundations contributing pivotal experiences to protection science, nature, and ecological science. Acknowledgments, for example, the Tyler Prize for Ecological Accomplishment and the E.O. Wilson Biodiversity Establishment Grant compliment the huge effect of logical undertakings in propelling comprehension we might interpret the normal world and illuminating protection methodologies.

Corporate and Hierarchical Accomplishments:

Honors additionally reach out to enterprises and non-benefit associations that show excellent obligation to maintainable practices and corporate social obligation. Accreditations like the Corporate Knights Worldwide 100 Most Practical Partnerships and grants like the Unified Countries Worldwide Minimal SDG Trailblazers grandstand elements driving the way in coordinating ecological obligation into their center activities.

Motivation for People in the future:

Past individual and hierarchical affirmation, grants in protection act as strong motivations for people in the future. By praising and publicizing the accomplishments of those committed to ecological insurance, these honors make good examples and inspire youthful activists, researchers, and local area pioneers to seek after professions and drives that add to a manageable and versatile planet.

6.3 Influence on Policy and Legislation

The impact of preservation drives on strategy and regulation is a critical part of forming the direction of ecological stewardship at nearby, public, and worldwide levels. Effective protection endeavors frequently rise above individual ventures, adding to the turn of events and reformulation of arrangements and regulations that oversee the connection among social orders and their environments.

Strategy Arrangement with Protection Objectives:

Powerful preservation drives use impact by supporting for arrangements that line up with their overall objectives. Whether it's the insurance of imperiled species, the safeguarding of basic territories, or the advancement of feasible asset the executives, the progress of on-the-ground preservation endeavors frequently relies on strong strategies that give a legitimate system to ecological security.

Regulative Changes Reflecting Preservation Needs:

The effect of preservation drives is many times estimated by their capacity to incite authoritative changes. Support crusades, research discoveries, and local area based protection projects can catalyze shifts in regulation, reflecting changing cultural qualities and needs. This can appear in stricter guidelines on deforestation, the foundation of safeguarded regions, or the consolidation of protection contemplations into more extensive ecological regulations.

Integrating Native Information into Strategy:

Cooperative protection endeavors with native networks assume a huge part in impacting strategies that perceive and consolidate conventional environmental information.

By recognizing the ability of native people groups in practical land the executives and biodiversity preservation, strategies can be improved with experiences that add to additional all encompassing and socially delicate ways to deal with ecological administration.

Peaceful accords and Settlements:

Preservation drives that work on a worldwide scale frequently impact peaceful accords and settlements. Associations and developments upholding for biodiversity protection, environmental change moderation, and maintainable improvement add to the molding of conventions like the Show on Natural Variety (CBD) and the Paris Understanding. These arrangements lay out a structure for aggregate activity and responsibility on a worldwide stage.

Public Mindfulness and Promotion Effect:

The impact of protection drives stretches out to the domain of public mindfulness and backing. Fruitful missions earn support for explicit preservation projects as well as make a groundswell of popular assessment that compels policymakers to focus on natural worries. This public command frequently converts into the fuse of preservation contemplations into administrative plans.

Chapter 7

Future Perspectives

As we stand at the junction of ecological difficulties, the eventual fate of preservation holds both commitment and intricacy. The direction of preservation endeavors before long will be molded by a bunch of elements, including mechanical progressions, evolving financial elements, and the developing comprehension of mankind's job in the complicated snare of life. This investigation digs into future viewpoints in protection, tending to difficulties, embracing open doors, and framing manageable ways ahead.

1. **Mechanical Progressions in Protection:**
   The eventual fate of preservation is profoundly entwined with innovative progressions that guarantee to reform how we screen, comprehend, and safeguard the regular world. Man-made brainpower, satellite symbolism, and high level sensor advances empower more exact and effective information assortment, permitting traditionalists to screen biological systems, track species, and answer natural dangers continuously.

   Satellite Observing and Huge Information:
   Satellite observing assumes a vital part in surveying changes in land cover, deforestation, and natural surroundings discontinuity. Joined with huge information investigation, satellite symbolism gives exhaustive bits of knowledge into the soundness of biological systems and distinguishes regions that require prompt preservation consideration. The joining of AI calculations improves the handling and understanding of immense datasets, working with more educated direction.

   Blockchain for Preservation:
   The rise of blockchain innovation holds guarantee for improving straightforwardness and responsibility in protection drives. Blockchain can be utilized to follow supply chains, guaranteeing the lawfulness and maintainability of

obtained items. This innovation can battle unlawful natural life exchange, advance fair exchange rehearses, and give a solid stage to recording protection exchanges.

Genomic Protection:

Headways in genomic advances offer new roads for preservation science. Procedures like ecological DNA (eDNA) examination empower the painless observing of species presence in biological systems. Hereditary devices likewise assume a pivotal part in distinguishing populaces in danger, directing rearing projects, and grasping the versatile capability of species notwithstanding ecological change.

2. **Environmental Change and Preservation Procedures:**

Environmental change presents one of the most impressive difficulties to protection in the next few decades. Climbing temperatures, adjusted precipitation examples, and outrageous climate occasions compromise environments and species across the globe. Future preservation procedures should be versatile, strong, and address the main drivers of environmental change.

Environment Versatile Protection:

Preservation endeavors will progressively zero in on advancing environment tough biological systems. This includes reestablishing corrupted scenes, upgrading the versatile limit of species, and carrying out systems that relieve the effects of environmental change. Safeguarded regions might should be reconfigured to permit species to move their reaches in light of changing climatic circumstances.

Carbon Sequestration and Biodiversity Protection:

Monitoring and reestablishing environments adds to biodiversity conservation as well as assumes a critical part in carbon sequestration. Timberland protection, wetland rebuilding, and reasonable land the board rehearses are essential parts of methodologies pointed toward alleviating environmental change while shielding biodiversity.

Local area Based Environment Variation:

Engaging neighborhood networks to adjust to environmental change is a critical part of future protection endeavors. Local area based transformation systems, for example, economical job programs and the mix of native information, can upgrade the strength of the two environments and human populaces.

3. **Protection in the Anthropocene:**

The Anthropocene, set apart by critical human impact on the World's geography and biological systems, expects protection to adjust to new standards. Perceiving the interconnectedness of human and regular frameworks is significant for viable and economical preservation in this time.

Metropolitan Protection and Green Framework:

As urbanization speeds up, protection endeavors will progressively stretch out to metropolitan regions. Green foundation arranging, economical metropolitan plan, and the making of metropolitan green spaces become fundamental for keeping up with biodiversity, working on human prosperity, and alleviating the natural effects of urban areas.

Manageable Agribusiness Practices:

Farming is a significant driver of living space misfortune and biodiversity decline. Future preservation points of view accentuate the reception of economical farming practices that focus on biodiversity protection. Agroecological approaches, natural cultivating, and the incorporation of untamed life agreeable practices add to the concurrence of agribusiness and biodiversity.

Social and Moral Contemplations:

In the Anthropocene, protection techniques need to consolidate social and moral contemplations. Drawing in neighborhood networks, regarding native information, and cultivating moral associations with nature are essential parts of preservation that go past environmental measurements. Protection morals that perceive the natural worth of biodiversity and focus on equity and value will shape future methodologies.

4. **Protection Money and Creative Subsidizing Models:**

The monetary manageability of preservation endeavors stays a basic thought for what's to come. Conventional money sources might demonstrate inadequate, requiring the investigation of creative models that influence monetary instruments, confidential area commitment, and new funding systems.

Installments for Environment Administrations:

Installments for Environment Administrations (PES) address an imaginative way to deal with preservation finance. This model includes remunerating landowners or networks for keeping up with or reestablishing biological systems that offer fundamental types of assistance, like water filtration, carbon sequestration, or fertilization.

Green Bonds and Effect Effective financial planning:

The monetary area is progressively perceiving the worth of green bonds and effect putting resources into preservation. These monetary instruments draw in venture for projects with positive natural results, offering a promising road for financing enormous scope protection drives.

Corporate Preservation Organizations:

Coordinated efforts between protection associations and corporate elements are developing. Organizations are understanding the significance of coordinating maintainability into their plans of action, and associations with protection associations can bring about mutually beneficial situations that benefit both biodiversity and corporate interests.

5. **The Job of Schooling and Public Commitment:**

Forming a reasonable future requires a very much educated and connected with worldwide local area. Schooling and public effort assume critical parts in encouraging ecological proficiency, bringing issues to light, and activating aggregate activity for protection.

Natural Training:

Incorporating ecological training into school educational plans develops a feeling of natural obligation since the beginning. Educated and engaged people are bound to pursue reasonable decisions and effectively partake in preservation endeavors. Training likewise assumes a part in molding future protection pioneers and experts.

Advanced Media and Protection Correspondence:

The ascent of advanced media offers new roads for protection correspondence. Connecting with narrating, computer generated reality encounters, and intuitive stages can charm a worldwide crowd, dispersing protection messages and motivating activity on an exceptional scale.

Resident Science and Participatory Protection:

The fate of preservation will see an expanded dependence on resident science drives. Enrolling the assistance of workers in information assortment, checking, and research extends the compass of protection endeavors and cultivates a feeling of shared liability. Participatory preservation approaches enable networks to add to the security of nearby biological systems effectively.

7.1 Ongoing and Future Projects

The scene of protection is dynamic and steadily advancing, set apart by progressing drives that endeavor to address squeezing ecological difficulties. These undertakings length different biological systems, include a scope of partners, and influence state of the art innovations to accomplish their goals. This investigation digs into the domain of continuous preservation projects, looking at their effect, and estimating the direction of future undertakings that will shape the eventual fate of our planet.

1. **Continuous Preservation Tasks:**
1. **Rewilding Drives:**

    Rewilding projects intend to reestablish and improve normal biological systems by once again introducing local species, reestablishing natural surroundings, and moderating the effects of human exercises. Models incorporate the Yellowstone Wolf Renewed introduction and the Oostvaardersplassen Nature Hold in the Netherlands.

    These undertakings add to biodiversity protection, biological system versatility, and the reclamation of normal cycles.

2. **Marine Safeguarded Regions (MPAs):**

    Endeavors to safeguard marine biological systems have prompted the foundation of Marine Safeguarded Regions around the world. The Incomparable Obstruction Reef Marine Park in Australia and the Papahānaumokuākea Marine Public Landmark in the US are conspicuous models. These drives defend marine biodiversity, support fisheries, and relieve the effects of environmental change on sea biological systems.

3. **Local area Based Protection Projects:**
Projects that draw in neighborhood networks in protection endeavors are acquiring noticeable quality. The Snow Panther Trust's people group based programs in Focal Asia and the Open air fire program in Zimbabwe are models of coordinating protection with local area prosperity. Such drives engage nearby occupants as stewards of their normal assets, adjusting protection objectives to practical turn of events.

4. **Innovation Driven Protection:**

Progressions in innovation assume a vital part in continuous protection projects. The utilization of camera traps, satellite observing, and man-made consciousness helps with natural life following, living space evaluation, and hostile to poaching endeavors. The Wildbook project, using man-made intelligence for species distinguishing proof through resident contributed photographs, embodies the combination of innovation and preservation.

2. **Future Protection Ventures:**

1. **Network Passages for Untamed life:**
Future preservation projects are probably going to zero in on making network passageways that connection divided environments, working with the development of untamed life. Projects like the Yellowstone to Yukon Protection Drive imagine huge scenes where creatures can wander uninhibitedly, advancing hereditary variety and upgrading flexibility notwithstanding environmental change.

2. **Preservation Robots for Checking:**
Automated flying vehicles (drones) furnished with cutting edge sensors are supposed to assume a critical part in future preservation endeavors. Protection robots can screen huge regions rapidly, evaluate territory conditions, and even track the developments of slippery species. This innovation holds guarantee for productive and practical preservation observing.

3. **Reclamation of Debased Environments:**
Tending to the worldwide test of environment debasement, future undertakings will probably zero in for enormous scope reclamation endeavors. The Bonn Challenge, meaning to reestablish 350 million hectares of corrupted and deforested land by 2030, embodies the aggressive objectives set for biological system rebuilding. Reforestation, wetland rebuilding, and supportable land the executives will be key parts.

4. **Metropolitan Protection Drives:**

With expanding urbanization, future protection undertakings will stretch out their range to metropolitan regions. Metropolitan protection drives include making green spaces, executing economical metropolitan preparation, and advancing biodiversity in urban areas. The High Line in New York City and the Million Trees Los Angeles project epitomize endeavors to coordinate nature into metropolitan conditions.

3. Cross-Sectoral Joint efforts:

Future protection ventures will probably underline cross-sectoral joint efforts, uniting different partners, including state run administrations, non-benefits, organizations, and neighborhood networks.

1. **Public-Private Associations (PPPs):**
   Public-Private Organizations will keep on assuming a huge part in preservation. Coordinated efforts between state run administrations, protection associations, and confidential endeavors can open assets, skill, and development. Drives like the Alliance for Private Interest in Preservation exhibit the capability of PPPs in accomplishing protection objectives.

2. **Native Drove Protection:**
   Perceiving the imperative job of native networks in preservation, future activities will progressively include native drove drives. Coordinated efforts that regard native privileges, integrate conventional information, and focus on nearby independence add to more successful and maintainable protection results.

3. **Corporate Protection Drives:**

As corporate supportability becomes fundamental to business methodologies, future preservation undertakings will observer expanded cooperation with partnerships. Corporate protection drives include taking on feasible works on, supporting preservation activities, and coordinating natural contemplations into business tasks.

4. Protection and Environment Activity Incorporation:

Future protection ventures should incorporate consistently with environment activity drives to address the interconnected difficulties of biodiversity misfortune and environmental change.

1. **Nature-Based Answers for Environmental Change:**
   Nature-based arrangements, like afforestation, reforestation, and maintainable land the board, will be fundamental to future tasks pointed toward moderating environmental change. These drives sequester carbon as well as upgrade biological system strength and backing biodiversity preservation.

2. **Preservation in Environent Touchy Areas:**

Preservation activities will progressively zero in on districts exceptionally powerless against environmental change, like polar biological systems, waterfront regions, and tropical rainforests. Systems for securing and reestablishing these environment touchy locales will be essential for worldwide environment strength.

5. Instruction and Promotion Drives:

Future preservation tasks will perceive the significance of training and support in cultivating a worldwide culture of ecological stewardship.

1. **Ecological Schooling Projects:**
   Coordinating ecological schooling into formal and casual learning conditions will be vital for future tasks. Schooling drives that bring issues to light about biodiversity, environmental frameworks, and protection moves engage people to pursue informed choices and effectively partake in preservation endeavors.
2. **Computerized Media and Preservation Correspondence:**

The job of computerized media in preservation correspondence will keep on extending. Future ventures will use advanced stages, online entertainment, and intelligent innovations to spread protection messages, draw in worldwide crowds, and move aggregate activity for ecological manageability.

7.2 Innovations in Conservation Methods

Even with heightening natural difficulties, the field of preservation has seen a flood in imaginative techniques and innovations pointed toward protecting biodiversity, re-establishing environments, and advancing manageable practices. These spearheading approaches mirror a unique reaction to the complicated interaction between human exercises and the normal world.

This investigation digs into the front line of preservation developments, looking at innovative headways, novel systems, and comprehensive philosophies that reclassify the scene of ecological stewardship.

1. **Mechanical Progressions in Protection:**
1. **Man-made brainpower (computer based intelligence) and AI:**
   Man-made brainpower and AI have arisen as useful assets in preservation endeavors. Simulated intelligence applications are changing information investigation, species checking, and danger location. For example, AI calculations can process tremendous datasets, recognize designs in untamed life conduct from camera trap pictures, and even anticipate poaching exercises. These advancements upgrade the proficiency and exactness of preservation examination and mediations.
2. **Protection Robots:**
   Automated elevated vehicles, or robots, have become fundamental to preservation observing and research. Furnished with high-goal cameras and sensors, robots can study huge scenes, track untamed life populaces, and screen changes in environments. Preservation drones are especially important for out of reach or distant regions, giving continuous information to dynamic in protection the executives.

3. Ecological DNA (eDNA):

Ecological DNA (eDNA) examination is a painless and exceptionally delicate procedure that reforms species location in oceanic conditions. By dissecting DNA follows shed by creatures into the climate, researchers can recognize species present in a given environment. eDNA is especially valuable for observing subtle or uncommon species, following obtrusive species, and surveying biodiversity in sea-going frameworks.

2. Rewilding and Natural Reclamation:

1. Rewilding Drives:
Rewilding addresses a change in perspective in protection that means to reestablish environments to their normal state by once again introducing cornerstone species, eliminating hindrances to regular cycles, and permitting scenes to develop without human obstruction. The renewed introduction of dominant hunters, like wolves in Yellowstone Public Park, exhibits the extraordinary capability of rewilding in reestablishing natural equilibrium and biodiversity.

2. Helped Development and Hereditary Salvage:

Because of the difficulties presented by environmental change and territory discontinuity, protectionists are investigating helped development and hereditary salvage methodologies.

These methodologies include specifically rearing people with explicit characteristics, like intensity obstruction or illness resilience, to upgrade the versatile limit of populaces. Hereditary salvage mediations expect to forestall inbreeding misery and work on the hereditary variety of imperiled species.

3. Maintainable Land The executives and Farming:

1. Agroecology:
Agroecology advances the mix of environmental standards into farming practices to make maintainable and versatile food frameworks. This approach accentuates biodiversity preservation, soil wellbeing, and the utilization of regular cycles to improve efficiency. Agroecological rehearses, for example, polyculture and agroforestry, add to both food security and biodiversity preservation.

2. Accuracy Agribusiness:

Accuracy agribusiness use innovation, information investigation, and remote detecting to streamline cultivating works on, limiting ecological effect while amplifying efficiency. By definitively fitting information sources like water, composts, and pesticides, ranchers can diminish squander and ecological contamination. Accuracy farming advances effective asset use, improving the supportability of horticultural frameworks.

4. Local area Based Protection and Native Information:

1. **Local area Based Protection Projects:**
   Local area based protection enables nearby networks to take part in and benefit from preservation endeavors effectively. These projects focus on the consideration of neighborhood information and connect with networks as stewards of their regular assets. Effective models incorporate the Namibian People group Based Normal Asset The executives Program, where networks oversee untamed life and get monetary advantages from the travel industry.
2. **Native Information Combination:**

Perceiving the significant biological experiences held by native networks, preservation drives progressively incorporate conventional information into their methodologies. Native practices for maintainable land the executives, biodiversity protection, and water asset usage contribute important bits of knowledge. Cooperative tasks that regard and integrate native viewpoints encourage successful and socially touchy preservation results.

5. Imaginative Preservation Supporting Models:

1. **Installments for Biological system Administrations (PES):**
   Installments for Biological system Administrations (PES) address a market-based way to deal with preservation supporting. In PES projects, landowners or networks are made up for giving explicit environment administrations, like carbon sequestration, watershed assurance, or biodiversity protection. This model adjusts monetary impetuses to natural stewardship, empowering reasonable land the board rehearses.
2. **Influence Financial planning and Green Bonds:**

The monetary area assumes a critical part in creative protection funding. Influence putting channels assets into projects with quantifiable ecological and social advantages. Green bonds, devoted to funding harmless to the ecosystem drives, give a road to huge scope protection projects. These monetary instruments draw in capital from financial backers looking for both monetary returns and positive natural effect.

6. Environment Shrewd Protection:

1. **Environment Strong Protection Procedures:**
   Environmental change presents phenomenal difficulties to biodiversity, requiring protection procedures that are versatile and strong. Environment savvy preservation includes distinguishing and carrying out methodologies that assist

species and biological systems with adapting to changing climatic circumstances. This incorporates the production of environment passageways, advancing natural surroundings availability, and helping species movement to climatically reasonable regions.

2. **Blue Carbon Protection:**

Blue carbon protection centers around saving and reestablishing seaside biological systems, like mangroves, seagrasses, and salt bogs, which sequester a lot of carbon. Safeguarding these blue carbon biological systems mitigates environmental change as well as adds to biodiversity preservation and supports waterfront versatility.

7. Conduct Change Missions and Ecological Instruction:

1. **Conduct Change Drives:**
   Perceiving the focal job of human conduct in ecological supportability, preservation projects progressively consolidate social change crusades. These drives intend to bring issues to light, rouse eco-accommodating practices, and advance mindful utilization. Conduct change mediations address issues, for example, plastic contamination, feasible asset use, and untamed life preservation.

2. **Natural Training and Computerized Media:**

Ecological instruction stays a foundation of protection endeavors. Coordinating natural schooling into formal and casual learning conditions encourages a feeling of ecological obligation. Advanced media, including narratives, online stages, and intuitive substance, enhances the span of ecological training, connecting with worldwide crowds in preservation stories.

7.3 The Vision for a Sustainable Future

An economical future imagines a reality where human prosperity exists together agreeably with the soundness of the planet. This vision rises above current natural difficulties, resolving interconnected issues, for example, environmental change, biodiversity misfortune, and social value. It requires an extraordinary change in how social orders collaborate with the normal world, encouraging strength, inclusivity, and mindful stewardship. In this investigation, we dig into the components of a dream for a feasible future, enveloping biological equilibrium, civil rights, and imaginative answers for the difficulties that lie ahead.

1. **Natural Agreement:**
1. **Biological system Reclamation and Versatility:**
   A foundation of a supportable future lies in the reclamation and versatility of biological systems. Endeavors to recover corrupted scenes, preserve biodiversity, and advance supportable land the executives add to the wellbeing and imperativeness of the World's regular frameworks. This incorporates reforestation

projects, wetland reclamation, and the production of network hallways that permit species to move and adjust because of ecological changes.

2. **Environment Impartiality and Moderation:**
   A manageable future requires a guarantee to environment nonpartisanship and successful moderation techniques. This includes changing to sustainable power sources, executing energy-productive practices, and embracing advances that decrease ozone depleting substance emanations. Economical transportation, green framework, and nature-based arrangements assume crucial parts in moderating the effects of environmental change and encouraging environment strong networks.

3. **Round Economy Practices:**

Moving from a direct economy to a round one is basic to environmental concordance. Embracing round economy rehearses includes limiting waste, advancing reusing, and reusing assets to lessen the natural impression of creation and utilization. This approach encourages a regenerative relationship with the Earth, where materials are persistently cycled and reused, limiting the extraction of new assets.

2. Social Value and Inclusivity:

1. **Civil rights and Local area Strengthening:**
   A supportable future is intrinsically attached to civil rights and local area strengthening. This involves tending to disparities, guaranteeing fair dispersion of assets, and advancing comprehensive dynamic cycles. Preservation drives that regard and include neighborhood networks, particularly native populaces, add to a more evenhanded and feasible connection among humankind and the climate.

2. **Admittance to Training and Medical care:**
   Guaranteeing widespread admittance to quality training and medical services is basic to social value. An informed and sound populace is better prepared to participate in manageable practices, settle on informed choices, and add to the prosperity of their networks. Maintainable improvement incorporates drives that focus on instruction, medical services, and social framework to inspire networks.

3. **Orientation Uniformity and Strengthening:**

Orientation uniformity is a critical mainstay of a supportable future. Engaging ladies and guaranteeing their full support in dynamic cycles cultivates stronger and feasible networks. Drives that address orientation variations, advance ladies' freedoms, and perceive the remarkable commitments of ladies to reasonable improvement add to a dream of uniformity and inclusivity.

3. Creative Answers for Feasible Living:

1. **Green Innovations and Sustainable power:**
   In a maintainable future, creative arrangements drive the change to green advancements and environmentally friendly power sources. Headways in sun based, wind, and hydropower advancements add to a spotless energy upheaval. The far reaching reception of energy-proficient practices in transportation, structures, and enterprises further lessens the biological effect of human exercises.

2. **Supportable Agribusiness and Food Frameworks:**
   Changing farming practices toward maintainability is basic for a supportable future. Embracing agroecological approaches, regenerative cultivating, and lessening food squander add to strong and reasonable food frameworks. Manageable horticulture adjusts the requirement for food creation with ecological protection, advancing soil wellbeing, biodiversity, and the prosperity of cultivating networks.

3. **Roundabout Plan and Mindful Utilization:**

Roundabout plan standards guide the formation of items and frameworks that limit squander and natural effect. A reasonable future supports mindful utilization designs, underscoring toughness, recyclability, and decreased asset use. Round plan disturbs the conventional "take, make, arrange" model, encouraging a more careful and supportable way to deal with creation and utilization.

4. Worldwide Coordinated effort and Administration:

1. **Worldwide Participation on Natural Arrangements:**
   A manageable future requires worldwide joint effort and compelling administration instruments. Reinforcing peaceful accords on ecological issues, for example, the Paris Understanding and the Show on Natural Variety, cultivates a brought together way to deal with address shared difficulties. Cooperative endeavors on a worldwide scale advance responsibility, information trade, and the pooling of assets to handle complex natural issues.

2. **Corporate Social Obligation and Moral Strategic approaches:**
   Organizations assume a crucial part in molding a reasonable future. Corporate social obligation (CSR) includes organizations embracing moral strategic approaches that focus on ecological stewardship, social value, and straightforward administration. Organizations focused on economical practices add to a worldwide shift toward mindful and moral plans of action.

3. **Grassroots Developments and Resident Commitment:**

Enabling grassroots developments and cultivating resident commitment are urgent parts of a feasible future. Neighborhood drives, local area drove preservation undertakings, and backing efforts bring issues to light and prepare networks for natural and social causes. Resident commitment advances a feeling of shared liability and drives base up change.

5. Strong Metropolitan Preparation and Foundation:

1. **Economical Urbanization:**
   With most of the worldwide populace dwelling in metropolitan regions, maintainable urbanization is a critical part of a reasonable future. Urban communities planned with green spaces, proficient public transportation, and low-carbon framework add to diminished natural effect and worked on personal satisfaction. Maintainable metropolitan arranging focuses on strength, versatility, and inclusivity.
2. **Nature-Based Arrangements in Metropolitan Regions:**

Nature-based arrangements coordinate normal components into metropolitan conditions, upgrading strength and biodiversity. Green rooftops, metropolitan parks, and maintainable waste frameworks add to moderating the effects of environmental change in metropolitan regions. Nature-based arrangements make better and more decent urban communities while cultivating an association between metropolitan populaces and the normal world.